W9-AFQ-300

The Pragmatics of Literature

Advances in Semiotics

GENERAL EDITOR, THOMAS A. SEBEOK

MARCELLO PAGNINI

The Pragmatics of Literature

TRANSLATED BY
NANCY JONES-HENRY

Indiana University Press

BLOOMINGTON AND INDIANAPOLIS

Both author and translator wish to thank Keir Elam for the generous gift of his expertise throughout the process of translation.

Published by arrangement with Sellerio editore, Palermo, from the Italian edition, *Pragmatica della letteratura* (Palermo, 1980).

Manufactured in the United States of America.

Library of Congress Cataloging-in-Publication Data
Pagnini, Marcello.
    The pragmatics of literature.

    (Advances in semiotics)
    Bibliography: p.
    Includes index.
    1. Literature--Philosophy. 2. Pragmatics.
I. Title. II. Series.
PN45.P27313   1987   801   86-45462
ISBN 0-253-34563-4

1 2 3 4 5 91 90 89 88 87

CONTENTS

Introduction

In a recent volume which offers an ample and perspicacious critical panorama of contemporary thought on the theme of "literariness," Costanzo Di Girolamo (1981) proclaims the failure of every effort thus far attempted to isolate the specifically "literary":

a) "Connotation" is not the monopoly of literary texts, but appears, in practice, in every linguistic act; and one cannot oppose, on this basis, literary language to standard language. The notion of "écart" does not meet the need.

b) The "non-referentiality" of literature is not a criterion of literariness: "The referential function can be slight or close to zero degree; or it can be extremely elevated, without a text thereby losing its literary quality within a certain social context" (108).

c) The concept of "poetic function," or of autoreflexivity of the message, introduced by Roman Jakobson (1960)—which in substance opposes the poetic to the referential function—is not valid, inasmuch as the literary phenomenon is in any case one of communication ("a message in function of itself would produce non-communication: the poetic function in the pure state is the inexpressible, a non-linguistic act")(110).

d) Neither is the Jakobsonian notion of the "dominant poetic" (1973), intended to resolve the aporia, valid. What is the dominant—asks Di Girolamo—of the famous electoral formula "I like Ike" adduced by Jakobson (1960)? "In fact," he adds, "with the exception of laboratory monsters, no examples are given of a linguistic function that is seen to be clearly dominant over others" (110).

e) Neither is the *Einstellung*, or "set," of the message an exclusive trait of literature. It is a procedure "common to any type of discourse and to any linguistic function, and a problem that regards the rhetoric of communication, that is to say, the setting of the message with all available, adequate, and pertinent stratagems: rhythm, euphony, alliteration, grammatical parallelism, construction of words, word choice, and so on. These devices can vary in quantity, but it would be difficult to do without them entirely" (111–112).

f) The notion of literary text as "hypersign"—with which Maria Corti (1978c, 89–114) develops one of Umberto Eco's suggestions (1976a,125–142) does not appear valid to Di Girolamo, since he retains that in substance it is still tied to the referential/non-referential opposition" (47).

g) Teun A. van Dijk's hypothesis (1972b) that the literary system would be endowed with adjunctive rules (rhyme, alliteration, specific lexicon, etc.), does not lead to any useful result given that "nothing stops such rules from appearing . . . in the publicity message as well" (47).

h) Neither is the Marxist sociological theory of literature as statement of cultural contradictions sufficient; though applicable to the nineteenth-century novel, it can be extended neither to other genres nor, above all, to other periods.

i) Then, the definition proposed by neorhetoric—that literature would be characterized by the "figurality" of language—is ingenuous, for, as we know, rhetorical figures are constantly used in standard language as well.

j) Finally, the concept of the literary work's "autonomy" is to be rejected: "One wants here vigorously to deny that literature, as such, is without any referential function; or that such function, when present, occupies a necessarily peripheral and negligible place" (108).

Di Girolamo concludes that one *cannot* define a literary text on the basis of intrinsic qualities or properties, and that it is "always the public—contemporary and/or future—which decides whether a text is literary or not" (109). "A text is 'literary' only if and when a public exists that is educated, willing, and competent to recognize it as such; the poetic function is not intrinsic to the text," but rather the exclusive result of the public reception of a work (109–110). If, then, one must speak of a "specific" quality, it should be specific not to literature but to "literary production," that is, to the fact that the work is produced by a writer competent in this kind of production, but received solely by consumers who—in this sense at least—represent an incompetent public.

Di Girolamo affirms, in substance, that what is called "literariness" is constituted by a set of pertinent traits chosen arbitrarily by the culture from the variety of a language's possible expressive functions, that this set, just because it is arbitrary, is a variable, and that therefore not only is it vain to seek a *quid* that is constituted within and "exclusive" to literature, but further that the only possible research on the "specific" can be no more than a "history"—a variable, that is—of the conception of "literariness" in the evolution of socio-cultural systems.

There is no doubt that "literariness" is a *convention*, but a convention that—and Di Girolamo would certainly agree on this point—one must not see, surely, as something established only by the culture of its "consumers." Original works always present themselves as "anomalous" in comparison with ruling socio-cultural systems; and on first impact, they even come to be considered—for just this reason—as *not specifically literary*. Thus they *produce* in the socio-culture the system of their "literariness," and only later come to be classified as legitimate components of literary memory. In short, it is not the "social system," but the work, that establishes "literariness." This point substantially overturns the con-sequentiality that one would have to deduce from Di Girolamo's thesis. But aside from this, is it really true that in the convention "literature" some constants cannot be recognized, some characteristics, that is, that in the passage of time do not remain the same? To state the matter clearly, it will be necessary to distinguish between what comes to be established as "aesthetic"—and this constitutes a very strong, funda-mental, and evaluative variable—and what comes to be established as "literary." To my mind, the "literary" has an infinitely longer duration, and even within the indisputable historicity of all human phenomena, has such "constancy" that it can be considered a permanent trait.

This "constant," it seems to me, can be recognized in a particular treatment of the communicative model, or, if one prefers, in an "anoma-ly" of the ordinary communication model. It consists in what we shall call *the introjection of referents*, which the patient reader will find discussed in the following pages; it is a kind of introjection that—as we shall see—does not fall back upon the concept of the absolute autonomy of the work, upon its non-referentiality.

This phenomenon—it should be stressed—can also be found in the form of a *treatment* of writing not originally conceived as literature. This does not invalidate the approach to the problem but on the contrary—at least to my mind—confirms its validity. On the basis of the introjective vision of a communication of the "historic document" or "scientific trea-tise" type, the former can be read as "story" or the latter as a "utopia" or fantastic "hypothesis," just as a sacred text, once held to be the word of Truth as Divine message can later be read as the word of imagination. These would be cases that Di Girolamo would point to in support of his empirical-variabilistic thesis, but to my mind they show rather how it may be possible to postulate a *constant convention* of "literariness."

In the pages that follow, I shall try to circumstantiate and make ex-plicit these concepts and others connected to or implied by them; and the discourse will prove to be as long as required to review substantially the entire, and quite complex, phenomenon of literary communication in its rapport with natural linguistic communication.

ONE

Transmission

0.1. Since 1934, when the psychologist Karl Bühler established the terms of communication in the triangle "sender/message/ addressee," with its three corresponding functions, "emotive/referential/conative," important findings have been incorporated into the model, although the essential articulation has remained unchanged. For example, it has been determined that the message, in order to be communicative, must refer to a "context," or socio-physical area, recognizable by the addressee. Further, it must refer to a "code," that is, the message must be codified from the beginning according to certain rules with respect to the semantic rapport of the sign's components—signifier/signified— and certain other rules with respect to the concatenation of signs—syntactics—and must be decodified, at its destination, according to the same rules. Finally, it must establish a "contact," a physical channel or psychological rapport, that effectuates the communication between sender and receiver.

The linguistic "functions" linked to the above-mentioned "factors" have been better defined: A function is "expressive or emotive" when the message centers upon the sender, "conative" when it is directed toward the addressee, "phatic" when it applies to verification of the contact, "poetic" when the message refers to itself, of the way in which it is made, "metalinguistic" when it is directed toward the code, commenting on it and verifying its use (Jakobson, 1960). More recently, scholars in the field of pragmalinguistics have published suggestions which we may confidently expect to complete the description of the phenomenon. To mention only one, Dieter Wunderlich (1971) proposed that the following factors must be clearly distinguished: (a) sender, (b) addressee (the two may coincide, for instance, in monologue or in the egocentric discourse of children), (c) moment of transmission, (d) locus and limits of the sender's perception, (e) the enunciated message in its syntactic-phonological form, (f) cognitive semantic contents, (g) presuppositions with regard to the sender's knowledge and ability, (h) opinion with regard to the addressee's presuppositions and ability, (i) place and space of the addressee's perception, (j) social rapport between addressee and sender, and (k) the sender's intention (including its communicative functions: "representative" when the sender informs the addressee, "provocative" when the sender requires an evaluation or a particular behavior of the addressee, "evaluative" when the sender moves the addressee to the spontaneous evaluation of something, the "expressive" when the sender moves the addressee to express feelings).

0.2. It is perhaps superfluous to repeat that the latest advances in communications theory cannot help but interest those whose research centers upon the phenomenology of the literary text, for literary language is, in substance, a phenomenon of communication, although a particular kind of communication that must, for this reason, be defined in terms of its own characteristics.[1]

Let us return for a moment to the communicative model in its essential outline:

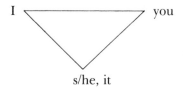

(a) "I" is the person who speaks—the speaker, or sender, (b) "you" is the person to whom one is speaking—the listener, or addressee, (c) "s/he, it" is the person or thing of which one speaks—the object. In comparing this basic model with that of literary communication, we observe a peculiar "doubling" at the three vertices of the triangle, which doubling constitutes the distinctive trait of the literary phenomenon. This particular question is discussed extensively in the following pages.

1.0. Let us begin with the sender. Is it possible to state that in literature the empirical subject can be identified with the subject who speaks in the text? The answer is that it is not.[2] This can be shown if only by the fact that the empirical subject normally nominates the text as autosufficient and absolute authority and thereby deflects readers' questioning of authorial intention. If anything, a writer often seems strangely interested in the various possible interpretations of the message, as if the text were not of his/her own making. Institutionally, literature is a communication "at a distance," even of years and centuries. No exception can be made, even for "oral" transmission of the text by its author who, in such a case, acts not as a normal sender, but as a physical transmission channel; the addition of paralinguistic elements does not modify the fundamental nature of the communication. Even if an author, physically at a distance, could be reached for possible clarification as to the intent of the discourse, s/he would choose to remain "absent," having established absence as a condition of his/her particular communicability and having founded the message upon an ambiguity that s/he does not expect to see clarified through verbal declarations of intent, but only through solitary interpretive processes carried out by readers. In substance, this speaker, at the moment of literary enunciation, has elected an "autonomous subject," definitively delegated to represent him/her, a "subject within the text" with whom, however, s/he has decided not to share the entire responsibility.

This separation has been variously noted by modern writers and thinkers. Stéphane Mallarmé declared that one can "have a human temperament clearly distinct from the literary one" and that an artist *makes himself* upon the page"; Paul Valéry affirmed that the author is not in reality "anyone"; Marcel Proust distinguished between the "I" of the empirical author and the "other

I" of the page; Benedetto Croce separated the "practical" from the "poetic" persona, and so forth. But this doubling had long been observed. In an earlier time, people spoke of "persona," of "mask," and defined the moment of creation as "divine furor," "enthusiasm," or "inspiration," imagining that the real subject comes out, so to speak, from the body and enters into a kind of trance, to become the bearer of a word that in a certain sense no longer issues from the body but from a different entity, often thought of as divine (the Muse).

The presence of the split subject confers upon the literary text a character very much resembling that of the antique oracles. One heard the voice of a human being, but supposed it to carry the voice of a god whose message could not be questioned. The word of the oracle had a definitive character, but the sense, ambiguous, sibylline, could be clarified only through the infinite and uncertain effort of interpretation.

Oskar Eberle (1955) explains this practice of electing a second subject from an historical-anthropological perspective. The theatrical manifestations of surviving primitive peoples, he finds, offer testimony of customs that go back to our remote cultural past. He affirms that the essence of theater consists in an individual who represents another I, who puts on a mask, and acts with voice and gestures according to the characteristic mode of a being different from himself (which can be an animal, a god, or another man). It is not impossible—and Eberle himself shares this conviction—that each literary genre derives from primitive theater. He distinguishes, in fact, between theater and drama, indicating that theater exists with even a single actor, while drama requires more than one character, each of whom establishes specific relationships with the others. The lyric genre, then, could derive from the single-actor theater. If, as Eberle sustains, the "mask is as old as humanity," we have the *personification of otherness* as a fundamental trait of the phenomenon we now call literature.

Psychoanalysis and linguistics have separately recognized that we cannot affirm the unity of the subject. Psychoanalysis teaches us that because of the existence of the "split" subject, discourse carries messages that are "effects of the unconscious." No longer, then, can we think of the subject as a being of absolute consciousness and locus of totalization of knowledge. The psychoanalyst usually has nothing to do with literature, but with the patient's discourse, and works toward a therapeutic goal that does not pertain to knowledge of literary discourse. Still, the split-subject phenomenon invests every type of linguistic expression, and in the language of literature, in which the subject institutes a delegated subject with whom it entertains ambiguous relationships of approximation and distance, it speaks a "voice" that makes itself programmatically receptive to every kind of projection and reverie, both of conscious order and unconscious nature, which is precisely the phenomenon once known as "divine furor."

Modern linguistics has distinguished the "subject of the énonciation" from the "subject of the énoncé," indicating that these are diverse entities, the one being the real subject, its nature shaped by individual impulse and cultural control, the other the grammatical subject which founds the law of the discourse and assumes its discursive function within the linguistic code (Benveniste, 1958).

Lacanian psychoanalysis has exploited linguistic distinctions to the utmost, carrying their assumptions to extreme conclusions. According to Lacan (1966, 89–97; 1977, 1–7), the subject constitutes itself solely in language, during that infantile phase when one passes from the Imaginary to the Symbolic order, which is represented by institutions, by culture, and chiefly by language. For Lacan, the subject is always, in any case, "spoken," existing within the "mask" that constitutes its only identity. This position, extremist and nihilistic, may lead one to question the idea of the subject's total destruction as an entity outside language, but one cannot deny that every type of cultural institution, inside which the subject inserts itself, constitutes one of its roles, and that language, which is preexistent to the subject, as are all cultural institutions, imposes its own law upon the subject, which is then defined as "subject of the énoncé." Literature, then, seems to *institutionalize* this phenomenon. It produces, within its own limits, and within the subject's consciousness *a subject of the subject*, avowedly offering itself as the convention of a discourse that is pronounced by a "subject of the énoncé" from whom the "subject of the énonciation" has taken its resolute distance. Literature, in sum, as programmatic praxis of the mask, institutes an imaginary subject whose oscillating relationship with the real subject swings between the extremes of strict proximity and absolute difference.

The separation of the real from the autonomous subject is responsible for the "universal" nature of literary discourse, which is the *voice of the human* as opposed to the *voice of the individual*. Literature is the voice of man's "oracularity," that is, of his "objectuality." And the idea, many times reformulated, of "aesthetic covering," tied as it is to the soothing concept of the autonomous subject, allows literature to convey (and to receive) "unpronounceable" messages, cultural taboos for example, and anything which normally constitutes an object of moral censure (Orlando, 1978, 1979).

So the corresponding process, that is, "decontextualization" of the entire message, is tied—structurally—to creation of the autonomous subject within the text. As we have seen, pragmalinguistic theory proposes the "place and space of the addressee's perception" and the "social relationships between sender and receiver" as conditions of communication. These conditions do not characterize literary communication, even though, as we shall see, the "social relationships" which characterize its formation should certainly be discussed. Indeed, a profound textual analysis which aims beyond a knowledge of aesthetic functions might recognize, and so legitimately appropriate, those "social relationships" proper to literary communication. The argument will be taken up again later, when I discuss the text directly. It is enough here to observe that the *readability* of poetic discourse, beyond certain conditions contingent upon its formulation, is a characteristic trait of textual autonomy, on a par with its readability through reference to the speaking subject englobed in the structure.

1.1. What constitutes this "internal subject," how does it appear to the reader's perception? While this "author" has not been studied as a textual element of the lyric, it has been the subject of close attention with regard to the narrative. We are indebted to Wayne C. Booth (1961) for the first ample discussion and also for probably the most exhaustive definition of the concept of the "implicit author" as a structural element that only rarely, if ever, is identifiable with the writer (73). Later, in the systematic research carried out by structuralist critics—and also in the labor of founding a narratological science—the argument was taken up again, to incorporate the "author" into a series of narrative "functions" (Todorov, 1967; Genette, 1972). Finally—to indicate only one of the major recent contributions to narratology, Krysinski (1977) has deepened our knowledge of the subject in research that must now be considered exhaustive.

1.2. What then constitutes the textual subject (apart from the problematic of whether and how much such an image may coincide with authorial reality)?

The textual subject is constituted by a complex of "behaviors" with respect to a systematics that makes up the set of social, informational, and overdeterminant rules. As Buffon said, *le style c'est l'homme.*

To return to a rudimentary classification that will, however, be more closely specified further on, these "behaviors" are definable in reference to norms and can be either *respectful* or *transgressive.*

As far as literature is concerned, the subject *behaves* with reference to two kinds of norm: *the formal systems of literature* and the *epistemic systems of the society to which it belongs.* These, in turn, form part of the englobing cultural systematics.

1.3. The empirical subject, too, is reconstructed on the basis of its behavior, but biographical research is necessarily based upon extraliterary documents and testimony. A biographer is faced with a delicate task, since the required objectivity contrasts with the fact that research involves material that must be interpreted. And interpretation is often bound to points of view, to ideologies, in some cases to prejudices, and even to moods. The first two biographies of Edgar Allan Poe, the one by Rufus Wilmot Griswold and the other by John Henry Ingram, who were contemporaries of the writer, even his immediate acquaintances, produced two absolutely contrasting images, the first dictated by spiteful antipathy, the second by apologetic admiration.

It is only later that literary products can be used to compare the two behavioral reconstructions, that of the lived life and that of the text. The comparison can offer the data to establish whether the two images agree, and the author has reversed upon the page his/her own real personality, or whether the textual subject represents an absolutely imaginary projection—compensation for the writer's failings, realization of a dream, or some morbid rumination upon purely personal aversions, and so forth. Only when extraliterary and literary images reciprocally confirm each other can we speak of an authoritative reconstruction. In any case, the practice of comparing these subjects (when it is possible—we know practically nothing, for example, of Shakespeare's real persona) is not to be repudiated. Structuralism, which has done so much to focus attention on the text, can be understood as a reaction against an excessive concentration upon the subject-creator. This exaggerated emphasis, an inheritance of Romantic ideology, blocked examination of the artistic product in its objectuality. Now, however, some material can be recovered, and methodological extremes can be moderated. The desire to reconstruct the real subject should not outweigh the task of recognizing the textual personality, nor should an overzealous scrutiny of the textual subject lead the critic to overlook the image of the empirical subject. A comparison would certainly be advantageous, for even when there is no confirming evidence of similarity, such an examination can nevertheless provoke useful reflections upon the reasons for diversity. In any case, the exegete's study is tangentially corroborated and illuminated, and the work assumes further referential values. This happens in particular instances, such as the works of Joyce, of Montale, or of writers of the last generation, in which the text is bound to occasions, to motivations, that occur in everyday life. These are cases in which recourse to existential situations becomes an indispensable premise of interpretation.

1.4. Umberto Eco too has alluded to the problem of the empirical subject, and he closes his *Theory of Semiotics* (1976a) with some thoughts on the "subject" of semiotics as one distinct from the real subject. He states that the subject of the expressive act "must be considered one among the possible *referents* of the message or text," and that "as such it has to be studied by the disciplines concerned with the various physical or psychic objects *of which* languages speak" (314–315). He then says that the subject of semiotics is "semiosis," that is, the "process by which empirical subjects communicate" (316). Eco does not deny—and this is obvious—"the existence and the importance of individual material subjects" (315), but simply sustains "that semiotics cannot define these subjects except within its own theoretical framework, in the same way in which, examining referents as contents, it does not deny the existence of physical things and states of the world, but assigns their verification (and their analysis in terms of concrete properties, change, truth, and falsity) to other types of approach" (316).

Nothing could be clearer; the necessity of scientific delimitation of the natural field of semiotics cannot be questioned. Now, literature too is a semiotic text, and therefore cannot have a "subject" other than that constructed within itself as "sign" or "word." But this is not to say that the literary critic must be forbidden every foray outside the text to research the states of the empirical subject. Literary criticism is not a discipline that can aspire to such a rigorous delimitation of its own field. Among other things, to practice literary criticism (a generic term, used here provisionally, and later to be defined in its multiple articulations) is to conduct an operation that engages human and social "contents," not only semiotic *mechanisms*. Further, when such criticism bears the appellative "semiotic," that does not mean much more than a reading which takes semiotics into account as a science of signs, and recognizes in it an important doctrine, a means to sustain its own discourse. Literary criticism—even when it merits the name "semiotic criticism"—undoubtedly includes interests that the formal rigor of semiotics must exclude. Among these, it counts an interest in the empirical subject and, further, an interest in the question of reference to objects. This is because literary criticism is not concerned with the *mechanisms* of signification, but studies those mechanisms in the contexts in which they operate, in which they acquire "values." This leads to considerations that reach well beyond the technical limits of communicative models.

Literary criticism, therefore, even that of a semiotic bent, will certainly have to study the "empirical subject" with the proviso that it must distinguish attentively between the subject that manifests itself *in* the text and the subject that remains *behind* the text. The lessons of semiotics confirm those of linguistics and psychoanalysis. They represent a warning not to take as given the fact that everything the message contains about its own subject is true of the subject who produces the message.

1.5. Again, we are immediately faced with the problem of literature's formal functions, with which, in which, and in the choice of which, the textual subject's "behavior" manifests itself. It will be useful, then, to attempt a *functional typology*, with the clear understanding that each isolated function which is recognizable as peculiar to a literary genre can nevertheless also appear, in the reality of actual writing, in combination with others typically belonging to different genres.

a) *The Lyric Function.* This function is of course characteristic of the lyric genre. The author-function—commonly called the "lyric voice"—is marked as the special competence to exploit expressive possibilities immanent in language. It is presented as the center of an exceptional "sensibility" composed of feelings which are not stated directly; rather, the lyric voice achieves its effects by means of rhetorical manipulation of language. It is constituted, then, by the physical-technical materiality of language beyond its practical function, its conventional association with signifieds. In the lyric voice, a possible language of exceptionally refined comparisons based upon semic combinatoria—the generic field of metaphor—can be created, to carry significations over and above its normal burden. The technical limit within which sense unfolds is chiefly the "connotative"; that is, sense is not located in the signified conventionally conveyed by the social association of signifier and signified, but in those subjectively experienced values that adhere to the conceptual sphere of the signifieds. Such experience, to use the terminology and the distinction of Gottlob Frege (1892), moves within the limits of the *Vorstellung*, which represents a function that is added to the signified and the referent as a personal, subjective contribution. Connotativity, as we know, is not a phenomenon to be ascribed exclusively to poetic language, given that it is richly abundant in ordinary language. Proper to poetic language, however, is the insistency of expressivity within the connotative sphere as well as the technique which renders connotativity explicit in environments devoid of situational context. The exploitation of language's virtuality occurs in a strictly "structural" sense, that is, immanent expressivity takes place only within and by means of interaction among internal relationships, within the rigorous compactness of the text's formal components. Finally, to demonstrate the impossibility of the absolute identification of the lyric I with an intentional gesture of signification external to the text, the interaction of textual components is also understood as the autonomous production of sense by structure itself, structure which has of course been manipulated to obey certain intentions, but which also manifests, of itself, other significations that are not, strictly speaking, planned. These other significations are made possible as collateral effects of language manipulation by means of forces which could be defined as accidental. As such, they are the autonomous products of language, and those of which the empirical author acquires consciousness become proper to him/her, while others transcend his/her acts and consciousness. The text always contains more information than the author can program or the reader interpret. Biophysiological-cultural energy engages with language as its *vehicle*, its *obstacle* and its *autonomy*. Language is "vehicle" when its schemata transmit impulses directly; it is "obstacle" when it is felt to be insufficient and poor, and the author is impelled to sound the unexpressed possibilities of the system, and does so principally by means of the rhetorical instruments which renew linguistic expressivity and produce previously unexpressed—and extremely precise—signifieds; it is "autonomy" when it induces the author to appeal to an irrational and sometimes fortuitous combination of elements peculiar to the linguistic system. It is thus that language becomes sovereign, self-producing. As we know, some theorists have been calling this procedure the essential poetic method (pure poetry) ever since Stéphane Mallarmé advised poets "to leave the initiative to the words."

We will come back to the problem of the text's "intentionality," and to that of its "unintentionality," which, however, involve considerations which do not concern the text *with* its internal authorial function but rather the rapport that establishes itself between empirical and implicit authors. Indeed, it is an almost perfunctory habit to unite the two authors in a single entity and to attribute every textual sense to its intentionality.

Let me remind the reader that the points I'm making concern phenomena that are not exclusive to the lyric genre. They can be found—and generally are—in any literary composition; here, however, the major concern is to construct a typology.

b) *The Narrative Function.* It goes without saying that the narrative function may imply the lyric genre, just as the lyric function may imply the novel genre. As far as the narrative genre proper is concerned, the "internal author" function is fairly well articulated. One must basically distinguish three different types of narrator, with respect to the position that these assume in narrative structure. The classification concerns the degree of knowledge possessed by the narrator with regard to the fictional characters and is now familiar to all those who have followed narratological research from the beginning (Todorov, 1967). The first type is constituted by the narrator who knows *more* than his/her characters (omniscient narrator), the second by the narrator who knows *as much as* the other characters (and is therefore a kind of character among characters), and the third by the narrator who knows *less* than his/her characters (naive author), who for this reason, acts as a "camera" placed before the facts of narration. Clearly, this various distribution of competence is a "machine" invented, and activated, by the empirical author; this is why it is easier, in narrative, to notice the distinction between "author" and "narrator." In some cases, particularly in first-person narration, we may be led to identify the two; however, we can postulate for the narrative as well as for the lyric that the narrative text, beyond its constitution as "machine" presents one or more narrators whose definite identities are recognizable as "functions" of the text, as well as a distant entity, difficult to grasp, whose relationship to the narrator (or narrators) is another subject of textual enquiry. The narrator is a *role* that the author excogitates and has his/her internal delegate assume. The "internal author" will emerge, then, in accordance with its role, as a subjectively abstract entity, thus giving the impression that the narrative tells itself, and/or as a subjectively concrete entity having the identity of a psychologically delineated person (as, for example, Sterne's Tristram Shandy). Thus, it can be presented as an extremely "competent" personality, on top of the situation, able to play the part with authority, to offer appropriate comments, and to make reliable judgments, and as an "incompetent" personality, confused, obtuse, destined to confuse the narration and to become the tiresome and often awkward interpreter of events and character.

Strictly speaking, the narrative function concerns the narration of actions from the beginning of the story to its conclusion, a level systematized in recent narratology (Genette, 1972; Bremond, 1973; Segre, 1974).

c) *The Descriptive Function.* This consists in the representation of places and of characters according to their "appearance." Such descriptivity, though characteristic of narrative, can be found in both lyric and drama. Eighteenth-century authors, and also those of the Romantic period, produced an abundance of naturalistic descriptions. (The English, in particular, have written poetry directly tied to precise geographic locations: the so-called *locodescriptive* poems.)

d) *The Directive Function.* This function is indissolubly tied to the narrative function (but it also concerns the arrangement of parts in any composition). Antique rhetoric included it within the *dispositio*. The narrator need not follow the action in chronological order, but can divide its continuum into segments in order to recombine them at his/her pleasure and thus to compose a particular narrative order, producing in this way analeptic and proleptic figures. All the effects of narrative time are to be considered within the limits of this function—attentively studied by Cesare Segre (1974): changes of pace, summaries, foreshortenings, ellipses, etc. Certainly, everything cannot be told—Henry Fielding declared, in *Tom Jones*, that his most sagacious readers would require a good twelve years to satisfy their urge to fill in the lacunae.

e) *The Phatic and Conative Function* (see, in particular, Genette, 1972). This function concerns the rapport that the narrator establishes with the reader by speaking to him/her directly, thus being assured of constant contact and sometimes establishing the fiction of actual dialogue (a device used frequently, for example, in *Tristram Shandy*). It is a function that works in the lyric as well and even in the theater, in monologues and direct appeals to the audience. In such cases, the psychological image of the narrator is evident enough, and the narrative voice becomes that of an affable conversationalist.

In addition to the attitudes designated by Genette, we can add others, stemming from Booth's suggestions, which fall within the same function. First among these is that of "irony," consisting in a game of hidden meanings with the reader, on the basis of which the latter acquires knowledge that transcends not only the characters' knowledge but also the explicit objectivity of the narrative.

"Suspense," too, is a most important control at the phatic level, insofar as it assures the reader's emotional participation by sustaining curiosity as to the outcome of events. Finally, narrative control of the reader's "states of mind" is achieved by means of those apposite descriptions which create a work's emotional aura (such as those crafted by Poe, for instance).

f) *The Ideological Function.* Within this function the narrative or, sometimes, the lyric voice directly expounds its philosophical, religious, and moral convictions, and comments upon action and character, framing one and the other within the parameters of axiological order; it often assumes moralistic and didactic attitudes.

g) *The Psychological Function* (not listed by Genette). Here the narrator is shown to be privy to secrets buried deep within the characters' unconscious, or, if the narration belongs to the autobiographical genre, told in the first person, it carries intimate confessions and profound self-analysis (i.e., James Joyce's *Portrait of an Artist*). In some cases, psychological inquiry stops before the mysteries of the human mind, leaving intact—not commented upon, not interpreted—symptomatic elements. This is how Melville presented Claggart in *Billy Budd*. In any case, we can say that the psychological function documents unconscious thought.

h) *The Transfigurative Function* (not listed by Genette). This consists in that most delicate overall operation that, by means of more or less overt allusions distributed here and there throughout the text, transfers the narrative's materiality to levels of generalized signification. These allusions are presented—when they exist—in accordance with literary convention. We expect from literature, especially modern literature, a further meaning that reaches beyond those signified on the material plane of sensation and event. The operation can be explicitly directed by the narrator—as usually happens in the eighteenth-century narrative and also in some nineteenth-century narratives—or the work can be presented as raw material of life, although it may be "oriented" or "predisposed," then left to the reader to complete alone the final interpretive task. Or—as in the case of Marcel in Proust's *Recherche*—the narrator-character lives the events of his narrative together with the reader, with whom he matures, little by little, some general convictions that do not have apparent antecedents but seem, at any given moment, to spring out of the shared artistic experience. Whether one speaks of overt or implicit activity, it is always a question of "overcoding" (Eco, 1976a, 129–135). The transfigurative function does not of course belong only to narrative, but to all literary genres.

i) *The Metaliterary Function* (not listed by Genette). This consists in a narrative discourse on the nature of the work produced, including thoughts upon its genesis, its value, and sometimes with apologetic remarks upon its fragility, its imperfections, and its insufficiency. In some cases, it is used for purposes of self-justification.

j) *The Dramatic Function.* This is clearly the function that the internal author assumes in a manner more or less constant in drama. We know that theater—at least in its classic forms—institutionally excludes direct authorial presence. The author is constrained not to speak in his/her own person, but to have the characters speak. The function of authorial absence is also a model of twentieth-century narrative insofar as it has rejected the omniscient point of view along with its implicit theocratic symbolism; rather, it points directly to facts, entrusting the work of interpretation to the reader's moral and ideological freedom of choice. It is evident, as Booth showed (and this within an ardent apology for authorial absence), that the narrator is always present, if only in material choices and linguistic "direction," in emphases. The so-called "absent narrator" is in reality a metaphor that alludes to a narrator whose morality is not revealed, who is not subjectively intrusive, one who evades the function that we have called, along with Genette, "ideological." The narrative that uses this metaphor conforms to the dramatic ideal (Beach, 1932), and is immediately recognizable in its various points of view. (Henry James was a master of this technique.)

The complex facade of the spectrum constitutes a polygonal vision of the world, respectful of its irreducible complexity. But not only is it possible to identify the internal narrator in the novel of authorial silence, of multiple focus. This indispensable being is recognizable, as the internal author, even in drama. Flaubert called Shakespeare a prime example of the perfectly dramatic author—one, that is, who always abstains from endowing characters with his own point of view, an idea reconfirmed by Benedetto Croce who spoke of an "exceedingly impersonal" author. All this notwithstanding, the immanent author can be discovered in the "style" of the piece (style in a wide sense: unmistakable rhythms of language, particular ways of structuring events, of conceiving character), and it is possible to deduce an internal subject who cannot in all truth be conceived as absolutely neutral or indifferent. The subject-function in the play's structure permits us to recognize what the subject loved, what s/he repudiated, as Booth established with regard to the dramatic novel. To illustrate this point, let me refer to Jan Kott's interpretation of Shakespeare's historical dramas (1961), his most impersonal, if you will, because they are constructed in strict accord with documentary sources. A Shakespearian vision of history can be derived from these plays, given that each begins in a struggle either for the conquest of the throne or consolidation of its power and ends either with the death or with the coronation of the monarch. Each offers the following paradigm: a series of crimes committed to eliminate adversaries; the vendetta of one of them—young prince, son, nephew, or brother of the victim—who returns from exile and gathers the outcasts about him; he represents the hope of a new order of justice and peace, but the process of crime, violence, and deceit recommences from the beginning. This cycle, which Kott calls the "Great Mechanism," is a criminal vision of history at the level of power.

1.6. I turn now to "behaviors" of the subject with respect to the other great systematics that is constituted by the *epistemic systems* of the period to which the subject belongs. Such behaviors derive from the subject's activity within the text's formal functions—now no longer considered as signifiers but as signifieds—and in particular will emerge from an analysis of the lyric, ideological, psychological, and transfigurative functions.

As we have already suggested (1.2), it is against the background of these functions that our identity as individual agents stands out. Behavior makes sense only with reference to a supersubjective systematics. Man is substantially formed of biophysiological and cultural elements, the former responsible for his hereditary information, the latter constituting that complex of systems that the individual inherits from the culture to which s/he belongs (family, church, school, etc.). These informants are slowly assimilated and in part come to rest in the unconscious, so becoming automatic elements, to the point of inducing the idealist to consider some of them natural or archetypal structures. What happens, in sum, with all cultural systems is what happens with the major (though not the only) means of communication and of presenting a world view, language, which rests in the unconscious as "competence" (*langue*) and manifests itself as "performance" (*parole*) in activities that are in part unconscious or preconscious. The personality appears in the *way the subject behaves* in relation to its basic constitution. Man is, on the one hand, "person," that is, we are individual entities formed by our values and the aims which we pursue; on the other hand, we are epistemic beings, existences immersed in a human world historically structured and organized. A major undertaking for a structuralist sociologist would be to study the "set of generative rules, historically selected by the human species, governing simultaneously the mental and practical activity of the human individual viewed as an epistemic being, and the range of possibilities in which this activity can operate. Since this set of rules precipitates into social structures, it appears to the individual as a transcendental law-like necessity; owing to its inexhaustible organizing capacity, it is experienced by the same individual as his creative freedom" (Bauman, 1973, 76–77). The ideas proposed of late on the question of cultural determinants should not necessarily lead to a totally deterministic conception of the human race, to the idea that in substance we would always react *on the basis of* overdeterminations. It is a fact that history moves, and moves transforming itself; sometimes violence erupts, quickly producing substantial destruction and restructuration. Man has obvious possibilities for innovation, even within overdetermined systems. But we must see the fallacy of absolute determinism in the same way that we must see the conception of human action as unconditioned liberty and as absolute creativity. The conception of culture as a set of systems, in large part taken over by semiotics, reduces the romantic point of view of ideal liberty, and full sovereignty of the individual, and corrects the assumption that the artist must consider him/herself as one who inhabits the void, and so must recreate the world anew.

1.7. The discourse on cultural systematics is flourishing.[3] I will try, in the following pages, to reformulate the theoretical framework, not only making use of ideas already suggested by various scholars, but trying as well to contribute unifying ideas and to sharpen certain arguments. I'll begin with a schematic formulation, then proceed to fill in the details.

1.8. Culture appears, from the semiotic perspective, as a system-complex (meaning by system a set of functionally interrelated elements, and therefore constituents of an organized whole, ordered by laws). These systems are as follows: ethical, ideological, historical, philosophical, mythical, juridicial, anthropological, political, ethnic, literary, aesthetic, psychological, rhetorical, symbolical, ludic, and so forth. They have a conventional character, collective (even though they do not necessarily belong to the entire community; in fact, each social group has its own systems).

1.8.1. The systems a) *represent the world* (otherwise chaotic and without sense), b) *organize both subject and community*, and therefore *establish norms of behavior* (mental and practical), and c) *permit communication*.

To speak of "culture" is to speak, *ipso facto*, not of structure only but also of structurations. The "structured being" and the "being capable of structuring" appear to be the two central factors of the human condition.

1.8.2. The systems present two "operations" (Eco, 1976, 32–47), as follows:

a) They establish rules that *combine* their unities (Eco calls this operation "the s-code"); and

b) they establish rules that *correlate* the elements of one "system" with those of another ("code"). Roland Barthes, studying the system of fashion (1967) indicates, for example, (i) the rules which combine elements of clothing—color, shape, etc.—and (ii) the social significance of clothing. Given the correlation among the elements of a system A with those of a system B, the system A elements become the signifiers of the system B elements, and the system B elements the signifieds of the system A elements. In this way meanings are established and become recognizable.

Such an operation presides, then, over "communication," insofar as it "constructs" messages (process of encoding) and "deciphers" them (process of decoding). Above all, to construct messages means "to actualize systems."

A "message" (which can also be an "automessage," when the sender directs the message to him/herself) is always a "text," that is, it is the syncretic actualization of several "systems." (The literary work is a macroscopic example, constituted as it is by a very parcel of actualizations; but even in ordinary language, there is the actualization of the "phonological" system, of the "lexical" and "syntactic" systems, of a "primary semantic system" and, occasionally, of a "secondary semantic system.")

1.8.3. In the modelization used in semiotics, a culture comprises, in general, three types of systems: (a) stable systems, (b) systems in the process of dissolution, and (c) systems in the process of formation and affirmation. (In addition—as we shall see better later on—it reveals a peripheral margin which is not yet systematized.)

1.8.4. The systems that form a culture establish three types of reciprocal relationships. These can be

a) *matchable* (in which two or more different systems can be considered as variations of an invariant, and therefore reducible to a single model). Lotman (1971) defines them as "structural systems."

b) *contradictory* (as, for example, the "mythic" together with the "scientific" orientation, Lotman and Uspenskij, 1973); or

c) *irreducible* (a plurality in no way structurable, which Lotman [1971] calls "mechanical").

1.8.5. According to the point of view of the person who considers them, cultural systems appear in "hierarchal" form; that is, they divide themselves into "hegemonic" and "subordinate" systems.

1.8.6. In establishing the terms "system"/"behavior" to indicate the rapport between the norms of the system and the kind of thought or action man practices in this connection, four types of behavior can be distinguished.

a) *Systematic*: Man acts in conformity with the norms of the system. As I've said, this behavior is often automatic.

b) *Variationistic*: Man respects the system, but gives it certain original actualizations, possibly even exploiting its latent possibilities.

c) *Destructive*: The system—even though this rarely happens— can be refuted in its totality. In political systems, for instance, this is called revolution.

d) *Substitutive*: In general, the rejection of the system leads man to hypothesize, or to effectuate, a new system. In art, hypothesized systems remain as a rule limited to the sphere of individual ideas, though the influence that literature exerts upon thought and on the inception, or coming to consciousness, of thought cannot be denied, and thus its eventual contribution in promoting action.

1.8.7. As Lotman and Uspenskij (1971) have indicated, cultures *autodefine* themselves by means of metacultural processes.

1.8.8. "Systems" can be classified in order to found a typology of culture. According to Lotman's definition (1971,1967,309), culture is the "set of non-hereditary information accumulated, conserved and transmitted by the various collectivities of human society," and because the set consists of "information," it can be studied as a text, "to which the general methods of semiotics and of structural linguistics are applicable." The specific task of cultural typology is threefold:

a) to describe the principal types of culture that, variously combined, give origin to various single cultures (according to Lotman their number should be relatively limited);

b) to determine the universals of human culture; and, finally,

c) to construct a single system comprehending the typological characteristics relative to fundamental cultural codes and to the universal traits of that general structure which is the "culture of humankind" (310–313). The *system of cultural systems*, then, should be derived from this typology of culture.

1.8.9. I turn now to a more extensive commentary on the foregoing schema. The subject can be "aware" of the cultural system, but for the most part is "unaware." Our own period is particularly concerned to discover underlying and unknown systems. Psychoanalysis and Marxism study, respectively, the unconscious determinants of the ego, and the more varied and evidently free behaviors of capitalistic society arising from economic determinants. Semiotics is now particularly taken up with the problem of revealing the set of various determining structures. Finally, the effort to bring about the coming-to-consciousness vis-à-vis a cultural system is often the task, more or less declaredly, and more or less directly, undertaken in our works of art.

The fact that the system can be unconscious is due to a condition that it will be well to remember when we make use of schematizations such as the above. Generally, man is not *ahead* of culture, but *in* culture. This means that it is not always possible to objectify and rationalize the operations proper to the history in which we live. Our behavior, more often than one would think, is comparable to musical variations—to give an efficacious example used by the gestaltists—on a theme one does not recognize. It is precisely the task of historical, philosophical, sociological, and psychoanalytical disciplines, and also, in their way, of the arts, to find the theme that precedes the variations.

To remain within our specific subject, let us consider the artistic system that is usually called the "period style." This style—as Arnold Hauser has said—"is a structure that one cannot deduce from the characteristics of its bearers nor by means of additions nor by means of abstraction. Renaissance style is at the same time more and less than that which finds expression in the works of the Renaissance" (1958, 232). The artist—also one who is most original and autonomous—is *within* the style, or styles, of his/her period, and moves there at first as within a natural environment. One can take as paradigmatic the fact that Stéphane Mallarmé, indisputably one of the greatest revolutionaries of literary history, composed his first lyrics in full observance of the Parnassian style. And we can refer again to the example of a system such as the ideological (to specify anew that every culture counts several ideological systems, which are tied to the plurality of its groups). The artist—man in general—behaves according to a series of orientations that seem perfectly natural to us all: to return to the musical example, S/he—like his/her neighbors—performs variations on a theme that is more or less unconscious.

To become conscious of ideology and of its limits—and, in the same way, of a literary style and its limits—is a process that is nearly always accompanied by discontent with a determined state of things and by a search, often neither programmed nor lucid, for changes that may lead to a more satisfying state. In any case, the same situation pertains to the writer, who works, on the basis of concepts and impulses more or less determined, toward the realization of a book. No artist can possess a work already formed in the mind, just as s/he does not always possess with absolute clarity the reasons why s/he is led to prefer his/her own values as opposed to those of the ruling system. The way will be uncertain and full of trial. And this is the reality of all existence. We live within systems that history has consigned to us and in which it has formed us, and of which we are more or less aware.

We move, because we are not satisfied, toward mutations that are more or less programmed, from which we hope to derive more satisfying existential conditions. It is the task of historians, philosophers, scientists, and also of artists to illuminate the unconscious systems that support a culture; in point of fact, it is impossible, within this perspective, to separate the work of those who in different disciplines and with diverse methods aim at knowledge of their own estate.

1.8.10. Cultural conditions (I am still following Lotman and Uspenskij) reveal three fundamental aspects: (a) *culture*, (b) *non-culture*, and (c) *anticulture*.

"Non-culture" is that which a culture refuses as "non- existent" in the image that it produces of itself. As I have said, every culture establishes what it is by means of metacultural texts.

The Soviet scholars point out that the image a culture offers of itself must not be confounded with the researcher's image of the same culture. The latter is an interpretation, therefore a model. (As such, it is difficult to see how the procedure can be scientific, as Lotman and Uspenskij claim.)

Non-culture is distinguishable from anti-culture. Culture opposes itself to non-culture as the cosmos opposes itself to chaos, ectropy to entropy, culture to nature, and so on. Culture opposes itself, rather, to anti-culture as a system of opposite signs that exists and is structured, even if the official culture refuses it (i.e., Christ v. Anti-christ). One could say—Lotman and Uspenskij write—that anti-culture "is perceived as a culture of negative signs, almost as though it were its own specular image (in which the basic elements are not overthrown, but commutated to their opposites). Correspondingly, from the point of view of a given culture, every diverse culture—with another expression and other basic elements—comes to be perceived as anti-culture" (1971; 1975, 55a, 79b).

1.8.11. From the technical-literary point of view, a writer who decides to produce a literary text is doubly situated, as follows:

a) *within* one or more stylistic systems practiced at the time of writing, and

b) *confronting* the over-all system of literature, in its entirety, constituted by its formal functions and by various concrete experiences of all periods. This means that we must refer to a "general system" and to "subsystems" that operate as intermediaries between the general system and its single actualizations. Sociolinguistics demonstrates, with regard to natural language— but the situation is analogous in every other system—that the speaker, whose every utterance always relates to an all-comprehensive and all-ruling *langue*, nevertheless possesses a multiplicity of other *langues* defined within that *langue*. As far as ideological systems are concerned, for example, it is correct to refer not only to subsystems but also to alternative systems (such as in the case of "counterinformation," with regard to the official culture). Returning to the practice of letters, its systems are the "formal" (see Section 1.5 on the text's formal functions), which supplies the rules necessary *to make literature*, and the "particular systems" of sensibility, i.e., currents of taste, which supply the rules that order formal choices and choices of content in order *to make a particular kind of literature*.

In any case, whether the writer conforms to rules in force at the time of writing or returns to the praxes of the past, s/he *makes literature by means of literature*. Gian Biagio Conte (1974) has demonstrated—with regard to Latin literature—that the Saussurian rapport *langue/parole*, while valid for ordinary language, is not so for literary language; to reflect the situation of literature, it ought to become *langue poétique/parole poétique*. It is thus that he could treat Latin literature as a praxis of "allusion" and "recollection."

"We do not know," writes Hauser (1958, 406), "what aspect the first artistic representations of things may have had . . . we know only that the artistic representations known to us refer to preceding attempts, because each such representation evinces several means of expression that in and of themselves would be comprehensible to no one."

Along with the overarching rules, then, are rules of taste and sensibility—the "period styles"—in which constant characteristics can be distinguished, either those of a formal order—in practice "choices" of particular "behaviors" in the heart of the general rules—or those of the order of content—in practice "choices" of systems as "themes," "motives," "plots," "lexicons," "ideologies," etc. The work becomes, in this way, a complex *montage* of systems—some formal, some not.

We have already pointed out that recent sociolinguistic scholarship has demonstrated that it is not correct to refer to a single *langue*, that one must refer to a plurality of diverse systems. For example, every social group does have its specific competence but there can also be—and there generally are—cases in which the speaker is competent on diverse planes. Then there is the alternative competence of the systems pertaining to non-hegemonic or non-official classes. The writer can present particular cases of poly-linguism, since s/he couples extremely various layers of language together with layers characteristic of the current stylistic system. Certain authors, such as James Joyce or Carlo Emilio Gadda, immediately come to mind as practitioners of this strategy.

1.8.12. The study of "literary systems" goes back to the Russian Formalists of the '20's and, according to A. Veselovskij, all these "material" systems reach back into folkloric tradition, and into prehistory. It is superfluous to recall—in this connection—Vladimir Propp's well-known 1928 study which, even though limited to Russian fairy tales, can be applied—and has been—to all other literary genres. In Italy, this reconstruction of systems (not to be confused, to be sure, with the traditional "source" research) has had revealing results (see, in particular, Avalle, 1975, 1977, to whom we owe as well a lucid theorization of the process, 1972). Avalle has declared that the great victory of semiotics is to recognize itself in the reduction of literary research to sociology; and, on the basis of the Saussurian opposition *langue/parole*, suggests that the activity of the semiotician be clearly distinguished from that of the structuralist: on the one hand semiotics, as a study of "systems," on the other structuralism, as a study of "behaviors"—a very precise division of labor.

1.8.13. I should like to dwell, for a moment, upon the concepts of "determinism" and of "liberty," which concern the individual in relation to cultural systems. Idealism, Marxism, and psychoanalysis tend to annul the subject. For Hegel the spirit of history manifests itself through individuals; for Marx, ideology holds man in captivity; for Freud, and the Freudians, the unconscious activates the individual; and later, for Lacan and the Lacanians, the individual *is* the unconscious.

From my own point of view, I wish to state at once that not even when I wrote of "systematic behavior" did I intend to allude to a full and mechanical determinism. Certainly, determinism cannot be absolutely affirmed, even with regard to ordinary linguistic behavior, given that the speaker who operates within norms always has the possibility of manifesting a certain originality of actualization. Even *within* the rules, there are infinite behavioral possibilities. The player obeys fixed rules, but the games to be played are infinite, and each one carries the countersign of an individual personality, of a particular style. Recently (1976b, 4) Umberto Eco has indicated that "the code, even when it is rule, is not for this reason a rule that "closes," but can also be a mother-rule that "opens," that permits the generation of infinite occurrences." In art, systematic behavior "opens" an infinitely wide range of possibilities to the original artist, especially when the subject sounds the immanent virtuality of the same system to which s/he conforms, thus enlarging its expressive possibilities (in the case that we have called "variationistic"). It is enough to remember that J. S. Bach was one of the most traditional composers in the whole history of music, yet none would dream of denying his great originality. The principle of absolute innovation, the idea of producing works with no resemblance to those of other artists, is of recent origin in the history of art, and even so, it is tied to a system, that is, to the romantic cult of personality.

Even in conformity with ideological systems—a conformity of undoubted strength and durability—behaviors differ in kind and number. The author is, as it were, trapped in an ideology, and often conforms unaware. However, even when speaking for and in the sense of the group to which s/he belongs, an author can be most original, even indirectly, as a revealer of latent factors. This is one of the requisites of great literature which, to be great, need not necessarily be utopian or reactionary.

On the basis of these considerations, we can now distinguish between *that which is systematized* and *that which is an act of systematization*. The "systemized" are cultural systems that the subject finds preconstituted and is constrained to inhabit; "acts of systematization," rather, are all those responsible behaviors that transform cultural systems or propose alternative systems (now generally called "antimodels," cf., Corti, 1978b). The history of science reveals that an original investigation attempts neither the organization of pre-existent interpretive systems nor their reformulation in more refined formal models, but to discover new heuristic models. The creative observer sees in something familiar, an object of common observation, that which had not been observed before. The subject is not only "structured," but also "structuring," a truth relegated to the back of the mind, or simply forgotten, by those who would indiscriminately apply the theory of cultural typology, the theses of linguistic determinism, and the psychoanalytic doctrine of the total destruction of the subject to "discourse." The scientific process is made up of continuous acts of resystematization of the material. And art, as an imaginative hypothesis of the world is, itself, an act of systematization. And interpretation of the world is also an act of systematization, not when it is limited to recognizing culturalized systems or projecting them into the text, but when it proposes an original hermeneutic systematization (if not otherwise than by systematizing the various cultural systems, historical and heterohistorical, into a single inclusive system).

It appears, then, that cultural systems are infrasubjective and passive, while the "systematizations" are original subjective procedures. On the basis of this distinction, I shall use the word "system" for everything that is institutionally systematic, and the word "model" for everything that is an original systematization.

With this, I'll leave aside the extremely complex problem of "perception," which closely concerns the *mechanisms* of modelization. I shall say only that, from my perspective, it is essentially a gestalt problem, and that every "observation," which is necessarily framed in some cultural system, is nevertheless transformed the moment it forms part of the "model," internally regulated by *its own* structural laws.

1.8.14. Lotman and Uspenskij (1971; 1975, 41–42a, 63–64b) define ordinary language as a "primary system" of modelization of the world, and all the others as "secondary systems," structured according to the language model. In other words, culture organizes the world structurally but needs a "stereotyping device," namely that constituted by ordinary language. With apparent reference to the so-called Sapir-Whorf hypothesis (1921; 1971)—according to which syntax and lexicon determine one's view of things—these semioticians declare that language transforms "the 'open' world" of *realia* into the 'closed' world of nouns, constraining men to interpret as structures phenomena whose structurality, in the best case, is not evident (42–43a, 65b).

1.8.15. Lotman and Uspenskij add that if cultural systems are structured like a language—and normally are translated into the system of natural language—they naturally serve to communicate. That is, they come to be used by senders to form texts and by receivers to recognize sense.

Stefan Żòlkiewski (1974) has pointed out that the two Soviet scholars do not deeply probe the pragmatic problem of cultural texts, and affirm, justly, that given that culture is a conflict of historical and social groups which struggle for a monopoly of information, a collateral and necessary study is to ascertain *who transmits the cultural text* and *who receives it* (including the "way" in which it is received). Such a study should reveal a dynamic image of culture, one closer to reality than the static image which results from the Lotman-Uspenskian systematization.

1.8.16. A contribution to cultural systematics, now under discussion, is the "theory of possible worlds" (Vaina, 1977; Eco, 1978; Volli, 1978), which refers to "possible states of things" and thus to conceptual schemes of competence common to a culture (Umberto Eco's "Global Semantic Universe," 1976a, 2.12, 2.13). Aside from the application the theory has had in modal logic, where the notion of possible worlds first saw the light (see Ugo Volli, 1978, 124–128; and, in particular, G. E. Hughes and M. J. Cresswell, 1973), the concept is applicable to literature, which is, by statute, a possible world. The Aristotelic definition of tragedy was not, in fact, the "description of things that really happened, so much as of those which in given conditions could happen; that is, things which may be possible according to the laws of verisimilitude or of necessity," a definition that coincides with that of Ugo Volli, according to whom the possible world is something that "is not, but could be" or better "is not, but—for all we know—is not contradictory" (cit. 136).

If, for example, we read Umberto Eco's most recent contribution (1978) in which he examines a narrative text, we gather that the "possible state of things" concerns either a series of possible characters, gifted with a series of possible qualities, or a series of possible actions (possible development of events), or a series of possible meanings for each lexeme. Such criteria of "possibility" help the author to construct a story and help the reader to read and interpret it. On the reader's part, the "possible worlds" are a system of expectations that in the act of reading come to be satisfied or frustrated. The study of possible worlds in literature will furnish a quantity of schemes to fill in the "detail" of the cultural system-complex. For example, what are the "possible worlds" in the order of the fantastic? Eco mentions the possible world of the fable, where one admits as "possibility" that animals talk, that men devoured by animals do not die, and so forth (see Schmidt, 1976, cited by Eco). And what are the differences between the possible worlds of one period and those of another? It is obvious with reference to character, for example, that possible behaviors vary in accordance with variation in customs and ideologies. A case in point is the difference in the portrayal of female character in the Victorian novel, on the one hand, and the modern novel on the other. Such considerations will also lead, naturally, to a diachrony of possible worlds where we can observe the metamorphoses of the frame of relative possibility.

1.8.17. Another important consideration: Lotman and Uspenskij specify that culture, while clearly structured at the center (polistructured, that is, in a system-complex) has peripheral zones in which "non-evident or non-demonstrated structural formations are gathered" (1971; 1975, 43a, 65b). They refer to the "recuperation" of this more or less amorphous periphery by virtue of the formation of "parastructures." The problem is not scientifically defined (cf. Cesare Segre's critical revision of Lotman-Uspenskian thought, 1977, 9, et seq.), but it is, however, fundamental to have established that the "systematization" of the world, a work of culture, *pushes itself only up to a certain point.* Lotman and Uspenskij state (1971; 1975, 84b, 59a) that the cultural system has two functions:

a) to describe "the most ample and extended set of objects," including "objects not yet known," or to declare "nonexistent" those objects that it does not describe;

b) to put order in the world of the unformed.

As these scholars suggest, culture "never comprehends in itself the totality of human facts, but constitutes in a certain way a separate sphere" (61–62b, 40a). We would therefore have to imagine a culture as a series of concentric circles, well structured at the center, and with external rings that are (a) "structured, but rejected," or (b) "unformed."

Let us leave aside formations of the first type, which are clearly alternative structures, "antimodels," expelled from the hegemonic system (not named in the metacultural autodescription), and pause to consider the "unformed" zones, which are fundamentally important to the ideas I am developing on literary work (and art in general). Beyond the structured cognitive sphere, there remain facts which are *almost known, imperfectly known,* or absolutely *unknown.* Strictly speaking, this means that a culture cannot be seen only as a "system-complex." The reality is that it is also constituted, and moved, by non-rationalized forces which *are* part of it in the same way as are rationalized forces. These amorphous forces can act and determine states and mutations equivalent to those that rejected structures can at certain times bring out in the hegemonic system. If these unformed forces were not to exist, culture would be more easily predictable and orientable. Even the central structures of the hierarchy constitute a difficulty, since these are, as I have observed, more "lived" than "objectified," objectivization being an *a posteriori* act. All the more reason, then, that the unformed circles should constitute a *mysterious* force. At this point, it is possible to attempt a brief analysis of these unformed circles to add to Lotman and Uspenskij's ideas.

The "periphery" to which the Russian semioticians refer could be constituted either by an "unconscious," more or less collective, or by "chance," that is, by material forces that consciousness has not identified and thus has not dominated. (We call them "chance" not because they do not necessarily have their laws, but because these laws escape rational consciousness).

Undoubtedly, the problems of desire are connected to peripheral forces. As Freud showed, man seeks *individual* but above all *social* solutions to such problems. He thought that knowledge of the neurotic illnesses of individuals facilitated our understanding of social institutions, in that neuroses themselves are revealed as individual attempts to resolve the problems of the compensation of desire that must be socially resolved by institutions (1922; S.E.XVIII, 235). The connection of that thought with the Lotman-Uspenskian concept of cultural systems cannot escape our attention. Cultural systems are structures that make sense of the world and that therefore render it "inhabitable." For Freud, the substitutive means of satisfaction in a social sense consist specifically in collective ideals—art, religion, and so forth, that is, the very cultural systems of which the Soviet scholars speak. What we have called "chance" can, with the progress of knowledge, reveal itself to be an actual structure, cognitively delineated. This has occurred, to name one instance, in the

Marxist discovery that economic conflicts are underlying structures, responsible for a series of phenomena (for example, alienation) that at one time were *felt* but not *explained*, that is, not systematized. It is in sum the case of once "fortuitous" elements subsequently drawn into, and absorbed by, peripheral systems.

This specification of the unformed zones closely concerns a certain operativity of art. The artist—who, among other things, does produce a text well structured (polistructured) at the center but with quasi-structured or unstructured margins, or horizons—*pushes the artistic structurization into the peripheral zones.* One undoubtedly important aspect of the writer's activity is directed toward the linguistic recovery of material that *exists but has no name*, and is constituted either by empirical perceptive data which find no place in the global segmentation of culture, or by soundings and namings that concern the profound psychic behavior of the subject. This operativity has not escaped Corti, who indicates that the artist has—among other things—"the rigorous destiny of ingathering the deep, indecipherable obscurity of the real" (1978c, 19).

1.8.18. A summary of the artist's activity vis-à-vis "cultural systems" must include *ten* possibilities. S/he may

a) actualize cultural systems (in conscious or unconscious ways);

b) combine and homologize heterogeneous systems;

c) intersect heterogeneous systems (one must see metaphorism as crossing of heterogeneous semantic systems[4]);

d) produce structures that are homologous to cultural systems;

e) detect the contradictions of cultural systems;

f) contest cultural systems (by direct or indirect means);

g) hypothesize new systems (utopias);

h) bring to the level of consciousness, one's own and others', latent cultural systems (most often accomplished by means of the indirect procedures proper to art).

i) propose, at the level of the Imaginary, systems to compensate for desire (utopias, fantastic worlds, representations of forbidden things, etc.), liberating in this way libidinal drives connected with cultural repression; and

j) explore the indistinct and obscure margins of the world (giving them "names" and conferring "systematicity" upon them).

A final observation: the artist's activity remains almost always, in its extreme subtlety, a circumscribed operation, one that enriches a culture's semantic system only in ideal zones, those partially, or not at all encompassed by the global and collective semantic system. Umberto Eco (1976a, 289) remarks that the global semantic system, which is a partial interpretation of the world, "can theoretically be revised every time new messages . . . introduce new positional values," but he does not say, and rightly so, that this happens every time an artist finds a "word," and discovers by means of the "word" a new and finer way to divide and to structure the world. Existential enrichment occurs *within the system of art* and does not necessarily produce effects upon the *common system*.

1.8.19. Semiotics has taught us to recognize in the structure of the single work many elements and structures that reappear in other works. We can therefore speak of "intertextuality" as does Julia Kristeva (1970, 67–69), and of "memory" as does Gian Biagio Conte (1974). It is possible—though rarely—to find some structures which are not historically recognizable, but the neological-reactionary structure always maintains a relation with the known structures which it totally negates, and for this very reason, the *known* structures justify its existence. I must add that in the history of art individual procedures are concerned with form, while in the area of content (above all ideological content) the author very rarely invents, even though we can say that a formal transformation always leads to a transformation of the world view, or, to put it better, a more precise "coming-to-consciousness" of reality. The artist gives expression to that which all the members of one culture—and other cultures with analogous problems—feel, vaguely intuit. Readers discover in the words of the poet the *felt experience* that belongs to them, though it was, so to say, in search of words. I'll return to this argument. It is enough for now to say that author and reader "realize" in the work the *coming-to-consciousness of their own feelings.*

1.8.20. We can now look more closely at the concept of "transformation," which makes sense of the way in which systems "change."

Systems are in movement even if, synchronically observed, some are stable, others in dissolution, and still others in formation. Some systems, those of *longues durées* (Braudel, 1958), persist for centuries, while others endure for brief, sometimes very brief, periods (microhappenings, defined by Paul Lacombe as *histoire évenémentielle*, cited in Braudel, 1958). With regard to the language system, for instance, semantic mutations occur more rapidly than do phonetic mutations. E. R. Curtius has revealed the constants of Western literature; Marx has pointed to the *longue durée* of capitalism, and so on. But I am discussing the problems of literature, and in this case, the dynamism of literary systems; therefore, it is upon these that I shall focus my attention.

The unities that the scholar of literature must immediately examine are those constituted by the particular systems that we call "genres" and "styles" (meaning by "genre" a unity such as the novel, story, lyric, etc., and by "style" not the personal style of an author, but the "epochal style," such as Baroque, Neoclassicism, Romanticism, Symbolism, Realism, etc.). Going back to the above-indicated opposition "system"/"behavior," we can say that a barely original work is an individual actualization of a collective system, of a certain behavior complex that has a social character. Of course, every literary work is, in some measure, *innovative. Absolute non-repetition* is its minimum condition. But I have pointed out as well that in original writings which are not innovative in a massive sense, but "variationistic," there is always some behavior that refers to a "theme" to be reconstructed. This "theme," not given but reconstructable *a posteriori*, which does not exist in a pure and complete state in any execution, but informs all compositions of a certain type, is the period style.

With regard to "genre," the "theme" is explicit and usually appears codified by a metacultural activity, constituted by rhetorical descriptions and prescriptions. There may also be metacultural indications of the "period style" in programs and manifestos, but for the most part it escapes precepts; it is material that comes to be rationalized after the phenomenon has taken place. As I have said, every author is situated, initially, within a collective style. It remains to be seen if his/her behavior will be a simply *variationistic* acceptance or will carry itself decisively *against* the collective style, to transform or substitute it. In any case, even the most original and strongly innovative activity *is possible only insofar as it is activity ensuing from, consequent upon, or in any case relative to, determined premises.* In addition, it never happens that transformations and innovations take place in all the systems that compose a text. No work, no matter how original and revolutionary, is new in all its parts; both original and conventional traits can be recognized therein. Therefore, even when a work demonstrates a violent reaction against a style, it is always *tied to the very style* from which it violently differentiates itself. It is precisely the *presence* of rules that confer a sense, and a value, to their *violation* and also to their *destruction*.

Such thoughts lead to an inevitable axiom: the liberty of the artist is never absolute. It always has to reckon with a contingent system. And not only that: the result of a will to liberty is itself recognizable within a range of limited possibilities. In the transformation of period styles *not all is possible*. The possible transformations are those that are *historically* possible. Hauser (1958, 305) has put this matter very clearly. He says: "Not only the individual's adjustment to a general tendency, but also his opposition to it, is in part a product of social forces. The artist creates what he will in the way that he wills; we ask only of what elements a 'will' is composed." We often say that the artist is a solitary worker. W. B. Yeats affirmed that "the work of art is the social work of a solitary man;" but "solitude too"—Hauser observes— "is a social category and can be tested only in a society" (305).

It becomes clear that one must see a work's originality as the combined result of individual and social forces. The most innovative work always meets definite cultural conditions with a definite individual talent.[5] To cite Hauser once more, "Neither the individuality and the particular talent of the artist nor the institutions and the traditions of his social milieu are sufficient to explain the singularity of a work of art. Not all is possible in every time, but even that which is possible from time to time cannot be realized by everyone; one wants the right talent at the right time and in the right place" (221).

1.8.21. I leave aside the problem of genius, and return instead to my argument. The question to ask is this: what are the objective causes of the transformations of literary systems?

First, it should be stated that two kinds of mutations exist—those owing to *external* and those owing to *internal* causes. I shall discuss the latter first. Lotman and Uspenskij (1971; 1975, 62a, 88b) observe, on the theme of dynamism of cultural systems, and speaking of the language system, that "if the inevitability of mutation, in the lexical system, can be explained by the necessity for language to mirror a different conception of the world, the mutation of phonology is rather a law immanent to the system itself." Later on they add, with reference to fashion:

> The *fashion* system can be studied in connection with diverse external social processes running from the laws of production to aesthetic-social ideals. At the same time, however, it constitutes as well a closed synchronic structure with a determined property: change. Fashion is distinguished from the norm because it rules the system not by orienting it on some constant, but on variability. In addition, fashion always aspires to become the norm but these are two naturally opposed concepts: it attains a barely relative stability, that only approximates norm. The reasons for changing fashion remain, as a rule, incomprehensible to the collectivity that is governed by it. This unmotivated character of fashion makes us think that we have mutation before us in its pure state . . . , a trend that manifests itself extensively, more or less overtly, in human culture. (62–63a, 88–89b)

This law of the autonomous internal dynamic is, as we see, extended to every systematic behavior, and must therefore include literature, as indeed all the arts. There is no doubt that it represents one of the fundamental characteristics of human nature, which is brought to change for reasons of mere change, at the same time that it is brought to conserve for reasons of mere defense or the need for stability.

Nevertheless, the internal changes of a literary system are also owing to a particular logic immanent to stylistic evolution. We must not forget that to make art signifies, in large measure, to resolve "technical" problems. The growth of a style is characterized by experimentation which involves a certain particular complex of expressive instruments. The growth and development of a style consists in continued efforts to refine its methods. When I said that an artist, though remaining within a system's normative limits, nevertheless develops an activity to exploit the available possibilities of actualizing the system, I meant to refer as well to this refinement of technique within a preconstituted range of operative qualities.

There is even a theory on the "saturation" of expressive behaviors, not due to external causes, but simply to surfeit of habit. Hauser cites the exponents of this "exhaustion" theory (1958, 251), indicating, however, that exhaustion does not always determine the birth of a new style. It is possible to find spurts of renewal in every area of taste, even the most defined and closed; nevertheless, these remain in the virtual state until some important external phenomenon arises that decides a radical change. The history of Romanticism is a case in point. Researchers have been able to find precursors of romantic taste long before the end of the eighteenth century. In fact, however, the romantic style exploded full blown immediately after the French Revolution and the consequent diffusion in Europe of revolutionary ideas.

1.8.22. Now to be considered are those changes due to "external" causes.

a) In the first place, such changes are determined by social and economic changes which usually lead to the appearance of a new public financially and culturally prepared to enjoy the arts.

In this regard, Sartre argued (1948) that literature tends to adapt to its potential public. There is another phenomenon which superficially seems to be the result of internal attrition, but which is actually due to changes in the socio-cultural substratum. It is characteristic of the history of the arts at the moment when certain expressive solutions and certain contents—the one inseparable from the other—are consigned to successive and diverse generations. And the passing on of the inheritance brings a sense of dissatisfaction and of inadequacy. The artist who receives these forms and these contents, and tries to use them, feels alienated. Hauser has clearly stated the questions that accompany a cultural inheritence:

> We always find ourselves confronting the same questions: Does the stylistic form in use still help us get our bearings in a world that has changed? Is it still always likely to provoke impressions, to convince and incite to action? Is it still a useable arm in the struggle for life? Does it reveal or hide what must be unveiled or hidden? (1958, 26)

b) In the second place, Lotman and Uspenskij indicate that changes are determined by, or at least strictly connected to "the expansion of consciousness of the human collectivity and to the general inclusion—in culture—of science. . . . Science not only enriches positive knowledge, but also elaborates modelizing complexes" (1971; 1975, 61–62a, 86–87b).

c) In the third place (I am still following Lotman and Uspenskij [1971; 1975, 61 et seq. a, 86 et seq. b]), mutation is ideologically determined by the contrast between representations and material conditions.

d) Feelings, it is commonly said, do not change; they belong, I should say, binding myself once more to Braudel's concept of the *longue durée*, to innate anthropological conditions. But surely the conventional manifestation of feeling changes; and our judgment as to which are to be manifested and which to be hidden, or which are to be privileged and which to be passed over, also changes. The reaction against Victorian literature was principally based on the open expression of feelings that convention had annulled in the sentimental manifestations of "civil" man in accordance with the concept of "civility" that the Victorian era had formulated.

e) I wish also to discuss "repercussive" mutations: Given the structural nature of systems, in which all the composing elements are necessary and strictly interrelated, the introduction of something new determines a destructuration and a consequent restructuration. Gianfranco Contini has demonstrated how this phenomenon works with regard to textual variants (see the various contributions of 1970). It is otherwise universally known that mutations within the work which regard the plane of expression unfailingly lead to repercussions on the plane of content, so much so that certain mutations of literary systems come about through innovations on a determined level of work which produce different mutations on other levels, thereby directly originating new genres. The combinatoria of elements and levels drawn from various traditions, diverse genres and styles, is one of the most common ways to transform literary systems. I have been convinced for some time that it is not the invention of new methods which enriches the history of Western literature, where everything seems already to have been invented. When novelty does appear, it is in the guise of *reexaminations* and of *combinatoria*.

f) Finally, but obviously with no hierarchal intentions in mind, the actions exercised upon the dominant structures of marginal and unformed forces must be taken into account. The phenomenon has been discussed with regard to cultural systems in general by Lotman and Uspenskij (1971). We have seen, in fact, that cultural systems are not pure structures. We find there, mixed with the factors of order, other more or less organized factors which hegemonic structures either ignore or relegate to peripheral rings of the concentric hierarchy. These "formations that surround the structure can become concrete as something that violates diverse elements of such structure and, at the same time, they tend constantly to become assimilated within the culture's nucleus" (1975, 83b, 59a). Such a phenomenon, because of the transformations or substitutions which occur, has a powerful effect upon the dynamics of systems. Naturally, the same applies to literary systems, as D'Arco Silvio Avalle demonstrated when he took up the discourse of the Russian semioticians, adding his own integrations and clarifications (1969; 1979). Rejected parts of a structure often combine to form other structures which may undermine, and even overthrow affirmed and hegemonic structures. The collision of contradictory elements within a system plays a specific part in this dynamism. Umberto Eco has shown (1976) how the dialectics of sign production and the mutation of codes is based upon the internal contradictory nature of the Global Semantic System. With regard to this subject, he recalls the Greimasian *carré* (1968) that, with its formal contradictoriness, is situated centrally within the life of meaning. And I have indicated elsewhere how the English Baroque, in the figure of William Shakespeare, actuated its own dramatic dynamic on some antinomies fundamental to sixteenth and seventeenth century culture (1976). Recently, Maria Corti has offered illuminating examples with regard to the twentieth century (Neo-realism, Neo-avant-garde, Neo-experimentalism) and to the thirteenth century:

Every society creates in determined moments its own ideology, from which are born some social and some literary models of the world. These are models of semiotic structures that can persist for a long time in the society, outliving the ideology that has created them and colliding with a new, nascent ideology. Thus, a conflictual semiotic process is created within the society and, by extension, within the literary system, and new structuring models, that is, new semiotic structures, are required. These coexist along with the diversely oriented structures inherited from the past. It is from this temporal juxtaposition, from the coexistence of the "diverse" in the culture and the particular and specific in the way literary groups and movements react to such diversity that fields of tension are born. (1978a, 22–23)

1.8.23. A conclusive postscript, to take up some already mentioned concepts that deserve to be remembered when we think of cultural mutations: It would be erroneous to believe that system transformations always take place in accordance with a precise, detailed, authorial program, the operative result of which may be in perfect correspondence with that program. It is true that certain transformations of style occur in the wake of manifestos and criticisms of the ruling system, anachronistic holdovers with respect to the contingent existential situation, but it is also true—as I have already said—that the artist, when s/he begins to work, is launched upon a teleologically vague creative adventure which is fluctuating, uncertain, made up of impulses and attempts, blocked by the resistance of the material itself. The actual results of artistic endeavor are unforeseeable, or only vaguely intuited; the execution of the work does not translate mental prefigurations. Its progress is marked by feelings of dissatisfaction, and in some cases only by the incentives of self-affirmation. In this way do the period styles move, since they too are transformed by the work of individual artists. Literary systems evolve in the same way that other cultural systems are transformed: Man thinks, programs, reacts, but results are unforeseeable both because the over-all complex of interacting systems is uncontrollable and because the decisive forces of history can also come from unconscious zones or, in any case, those zones peripheral to a culture's rationalized center.

1.9. It is necessary now to add some further observations to complete the phenomenological framework of literary transmission. I have said that in the ordinary communication model, for communication to take place, both sender and addressee must refer to the same code (that is, to the same correlations of signifiers and signifieds). In the literary phenomenon, the problem is not so simple as its scientific formulation, based upon the facts of ordinary communication, would indicate. Undoubtedly, reference to systems also takes place in literature. But the great difference lies in the fact (a) that literature refers to a relevant complexity of systems as opposed to the simple reference that characterizes ordinary communication; (b) that some of these systems are not immediately accessible; and (c) that still others are not given but are nevertheless reconstructible within and by means of the text (perhaps, as more often happens, within the context of an author's entire *oeuvre*, considered as a macrotext). This systematic complexity does include literature in the general law of communication; it presupposes, however, a range of competence on the part of the addressee that, in the majority of cases, reaches an extremely high level of expertise. This requires, with only a few exceptions which I shall mention immediately, a norm with respect to *otherness*, but with a concept of *alterity* very different from that of ordinary communication.

This means, yet again, that the expressive impulse does not pass directly into the text but arrives there by way of, and shaped by, linguistic systems and fraught with complex presuppositions about the possibility of comprehension by the addressee. The Romantic-Idealistic aesthetic often refers to authors who write *only for themselves*. This would be, then, in related poetics, the matrix of genuine expression. In reality, the poet *never* writes for him/herself; or better, s/he does write for her/himself insofar as the *self* is the ideal constitution of the image of the *other*. It is a law of language, or better of the subject's foundation in language—studied with extreme clarity by Emile Benveniste (1966, Chapters V and VIII)—that the subject constitutes itself in language "which calls upon the 'other' to verify it." The message without otherness is—as demonstrated in schizophrenic language—a message without communication. Jacques Lacan has described the infantile process of splitting and identification of the subject during the "mirror stage." In the literary phenomenon, which repeats practically the same process, the author selects some cultural systems as points of reference, and does so in function of their availability/non-availability to the "other." One can say that there is an exception only in *symbolist* and *post-symbolist* poetry, which represents a voluntary separation from the ordinary reader; but this is, however, a partial exception, because in this limited case too a rare and exceptional reader is postulated, one who, up to a certain level of competence, can reconstruct the sense, and also change the "non-sense" into something that is, ultimately, a "sense." It is a question, in substance, of a phenomenon that exalts one aspect of all literature, which does not exhaust itself, among other things, in its communicative intentionality.

1.10. The parabola of my discourse has necessarily been long. I can now return to the point of departure and conclude. Knowledge of cultural complexes constitutes an indispensable element, concrete and objective, in the identification of the physiognomy both of the textual author and of the empirical author, each being structured by the systems in question and each being constrained to manifest itself either within, or in any case with reference to these systems in all its behavior, even the most original and emancipating. I have also shown that identification of the internal subject's behavior constitutes the primary interest of the addressee of literature, but I have indicated as well the usefulness of a comparison of the image of the textual subject with that of the empirical subject (where the comparison is possible). And finally, I have verified that, by means of the knowledge of systems, one can make a definitely more useful comparison between the textual subject and *all* the empirical subjects in the social reality of a given culture, who represent the *normality* against which the *values* of artistic behavior stand out.

From psychoanalytic inquiries we might also expect an analogous configuration of relationships. It is not the real author's psychological make-up which should interest the psychoanalytically inclined literary critic but rather the rapport that psychoanalytic models, drawn from the work, establish with a cultural psychoanalytic typology, a kind of period psychoanalysis that offers a picture of the collective psychic state in a given historical period. It seems to me, however, that the idea of this kind of psychoanalysis might have been what Freud had in his mind during the final phase of the development of his thought—the Freud of *Civilization and Its Discontents*.

TWO

Reception

2.0. The argument I've been developing in the preceding section on the alterity of both literary and non-literary messages now leads me to a series of observations with regard to the "addressee."

We have seen that the Bühler triangle, applied to literature, would manifest characteristic "doublings" or "introjections" at its vertices. Now, symmetrical to the doubling of internal and external senders, there is the doubling of internal and external addressees.[1] The author not only elects his or her own delegate within the text but prefigures the reader who will necessarily receive its message. This phenomenon had already been observed by the sociologists of literature. Sartre, for example, had said that "all works of the spirit contain within themselves the image of the reader to whom they are addressed" (1948, 92).

But this is not to say—as Sartre knew—that only one reader is projected by the author in the act of formulating the discourse; rather, there are at least three types of prefigured reader, which we shall now examine.

2.1. In the first case, the author conceives the reader as prototype of a determined social class, possessed of a given culture, a particular sensibility, and a particular taste. Often, but not necessarily, such an individual is conceived to be in possession of the same perceptive sophistication and the same cultural systems as the author (those proper to literature as well as axiological and ideological systems). This is true whether the author is prepared to treat the reader sympathetically or whether s/he wishes to confute principles, modify thought, and, sometimes, even modes of behavior. We can define this fundamental type of internal addressee as the "ideal reader" (Eco's "Model Reader," 1978). The eighteenth-century novel offers a limited example: a bourgeois writer elects a public of bourgeois readers, those who have attended the same schools, read the same books, hold the same ideological convictions, and so on. With this type of reader in mind, s/he hypothesizes particular linguistic contacts, and then a particular type of diction, and establishes particular expressive materials. Sartre wrote that it is "the choice that an author makes of a certain aspect of the world that determines the reader and, reciprocally, the choice of the reader that determines the subject" (1948, 91–92). By presupposing in the addressee a determined type of cultural formation, the author is permitted particular allusions, particular ellipses. All cannot be stated in the discourse, and while the stated and the suppressed do respond to some choices of an aesthetic order, there is also a precise logic of statement and suppression in a given rapport that the text establishes with the idea of its addressee.

2.2. Next to this clearly delineated reader there is generally another, who, with Sartre, I shall call the "potential" reader. This is a different reader, of a different culture, belonging to a different social class. In general, this potentiality is cultivated, perhaps not at once, by those writers—especially novelists—who belong to a historical period in which a rising social class is clearly in evidence. It was thus that at the beginning of the eighteenth century, coinciding with the advent of the bourgeois class, polite literature did not treat exclusively of elite characters, but endeavoured to address itself as well to the bourgeoisie which was beginning to produce a conspicuous reading public. In the years that followed World War II, Sartre was remonstrating with European writers for not recognizing the new historical reality, constituted by the birth of a proletarian public. The situation, here, was different from that of the eighteenth-century authors, consisting as it did in the refusal to communicate with even the middle bourgeoisie; by now, further changes have occurred: the "mass" reader has appeared on history's horizon,[2] and it was inevitable that writers should exist who not only presupposed this reader as virtuality, but who directly fixed upon the "mass" as the ideal reader.

2.3. Beyond the horizon of the "potential" reader we must recognize that there is a third reader—considered by Sartre, but overlooked, in general, by the sociologists of literature—that we could call "universal." In brief, this reader, constituted abstractly by "humanity," is tied to the ambition, always manifest in writers, to live beyond one's own time, to gain, by virtue of the future readability of one's own products, a kind of immortality. This type of reader, too, is based upon presuppositions. The idealist writer counts on what s/he calls "human universals," and if s/he is materialist, on the *longues durées* of culture, among which, above all, are those relative universals constituted by anthropological traits. It is on the basis of fundamental human systems that the antique Greek theater continues to be an important communicative phenomenon, even though our comprehension is deficient—most of the necessary codes are lost to us.

2.4. We can, of course, subclassify this essential typology of literature's addressees. In some cases the author's image of the addressee can be typologically more selective. According to Sartre, the black American writer Richard Wright addressed his message primarily to the cultivated Northern negro and secondarily to liberal white Americans. There can be readers chosen from groups held together by diverse factors, not only race, for example, but also ideology—groups formed on the basis of religious, political, or even sexual identity. We know that a vast "women's" literature exists, which has its roots in the Middle Ages, and which, as Levin L. Schücking (1961) observes, continues throughout the Baroque Age, the eighteenth century—witness Samuel Richardson—and also the Romantic period, not excluding sentimental narrative poems such as those of Lord Byron. Usually, "masculine" literature has an intellectual-philosophical bent. In addition, there is a "children's" literature, an "adult" literature—in general conservative—and an "avant-garde" literature, which is generally intellectually adventurous, progressive, desecrator of consolidated ideals, inclined toward radical changes in taste. Then, a "middle-brow" literature, widespread in the nineteenth century when books were read aloud to the whole family, maintains an equilibrium among diverse kinds of readers. We are now producing a "feminist" literature. And so it goes.

2.5. The final distinction to be made is that between "ordinary" and "specialist" reading. An "ordinary" reading seeks event, experience, and identification with characters, sometimes to a high degree of empathy; it is not as a rule concerned with formal questions. In the best case, an "ordinary" reader may experience through literature some "coming to consciousness" of his/her own existential state. As a "type" this reader is intellectually lazy, one who refuses the effort of profound reading when the page demands a stronger commitment. S/he has acquired a "competence," and expects literature always faithfully to actualize it. In sum, s/he is a conserver of tastes, of ideas, of customs. As we know, during the second half of the nineteenth century the most highly qualified literateurs reacted against this reader—bourgeois by definition—thus bringing about the rupture we've been discussing.

2.6. Opposed to the "ordinary" is the "specialist" reading, which I shall discuss extensively later on, to illustrate its multiple activities. It too forms categories on the basis of the reader's theoretical and ideological convictions. (This reader could be an historicist, an idealist, a formalist, a structuralist, a Marxist, and so on.) In conformity with his or her own mental constructs, this reader expects from the message certain determined contents and certain determined forms. In general, a specialist reading is devoted to the text's connotative levels, to the most astonishing hermeneutics. Most symptomatically, Greimas has said that aesthetic pleasure—he means for our elite reader—consists in the discovery of hidden isotopies.

Writers may also elect the specialist as the only implicit addressee, but generally they place him/her beside one or more less exigent readers and situate him/her within a perspective further from the virtual reading. The Symbolists, however, made an exclusive election; they addressed their literature to the most restricted and select circles of personal friends, or in any case to especially qualified readers. During the entire first half of the twentieth century, the lyric, and in some cases the narrative as well, continued to be jealous, cryptic expressions, addressed to the "happy few."

2.7. Not all literary works have projected an adequate "specialist" reader as implicit addressee. While the formula that every work contains the image of its reader remains valid, this image may *anticipate* its own existence in real time. Truly original works, those which are most at odds with acquired and ruling systems, are not immediately understood. In our century, new work is always axiomatically conceived as violent rupture with preceding works. A Gertrude Stein statement is emblematic: "If it has a public, it isn't art." The work is partially, or even completely, incomprehensible at the first reading, even to the specialist reader. Step by step, however, the exegete unravels the textual tangle, isolates its technique, and puts its sense in evidence. Often years go by before this work is finished: *Finnegans Wake* has not yet been completely assimilated; we are very far from understanding—to mention other work—Thomas Pynchon's novels (in particular *Gravity's Rainbow*, 1973). The specialist reader acquires, through the work, an *ad hoc* specialization. In such cases it is not the addressee which determines a particular work, but the work which generates its own readers. Still emblematically— and to remain at Montparnasse in the years of the twentieth-century avant-garde—we quote Picasso. To someone who observed that his portrait of Stein did not look like her, the artist replied "It will!" In some cases, one generation does not suffice for a work to become fully understood and appreciated. Capillary exegetic work is required, and with it the slow formation of a particular taste.

2.8. Until now I have referred to addressees as "prefigurations." They are, as we have seen, *schematic* entities, ideally conceived by the writer, and they become textual "functions." The literary text, constructed on the ordinary communication model but differing from that model by reason of a series of its own characteristics, is inconceivable without the possibility of an ideal reception. But readers, in their reality as "empirical receivers," are subjective, singularly unidentifiable individuals who may also belong to diverse epochs and therefore to cultures extremely distant from those that characterize the transmission.

Most recent linguistics—under the aegis of *Textlinguistik*—indicates that in ordinary communication the addressee is located in a series of "presuppositions," listed below (Siegfried J. Schmidt, in Maria-Elisabeth Conte, 1977, 254):

a) *socio-economic* (that is, the addressee's role (status) and economic position);

b) *socio-cultural* and *cognitive-intellectual* (degree of knowledge of linguistic textuality, level of education, experience, and social sophistication);

c) *biographical-psychical* (motivations, personal dispositions);

d) *linguistic-communicative* (degree of knowledge of the code, mastery of communicative rules; in a word, "competence" with regard to the practice of communication).

It is evident that the sender of the literary text cannot have in mind such a concrete, definite image of the empirical receiver. Indeed, it is rare to find a text directed to a single real person, though Shakespeare's *Sonnets* were placed directly into the hands of their dedicatee, the Earl of Southampton, and many of Emily Dickinson's poems were handwritten to her sister-in-law Susan Gilbert. Even these compositions, though, must have contained some implicit, ideally conceived addressees, and must have directly presupposed some universal readers. Keeping in mind the ideas that I was developing at the beginning of this discourse, we can say that the fundamental difference between ordinary and literary communication rests in the fact that the latter *is not in situation*. Therefore, the literary text carries, among its countersigns, a constitution which permits an ideal recontextualization due to the introjection of referential elements which in ordinary linguistic praxis are taken as understood or signified—insofar as they are materially present—by means of deictic processes. Literary language plays upon its characteristic decontextuality/recontextuability for effects that aim at a non-contingent comprehension, generator of an oracular and universal statute. The limited case is described by Jean Starobinski in his reflection on a passage from the Gospels (Mark, v, 1–20):

> To which author (or speaker) does the text belong? It is not the first-person author. . . . The text is not then produced by the thought, the will, the memory, the uncertainties of an individual. The "narrator" is completely suppressed, as if to subtract from the work everything that would relate it to a single person, that would depend upon a particular point of view, not be cause of modesty, but to confer upon the story the authority of absolute knowledge. We find before us the type of pure narrative, which functions radically to exclude every significant reference to the author. There is space only for the designation of a "referent" (the life and Passion of Jesus) to which is tied the destiny of humanity. . . . The text does not explicitly mention any addressee. It is not made final in a determined way; only by recourse to scattered hints can we conjecture that the Gospel of Mark "originally" refers to a paleochristian community. But the absence of a determined addressee allows the addressee to be universal. The narrative devoid of shadows calls for a reading identification by everyone, in every age. Christ, addressing His listeners within the narrative's definite circumstances, reaches the future reader either because His words are so general that they reach beyond the occasion that has provoked them, or because the episodes consist of acts which cover a symbolic function to which the readers of any age can respond (1974, 78–82).

In the literary communication model, then, "doubling" occurs also at the text's destination, a doubling that contemplates on the one hand the "internal addressee" (who, as we have seen, can be composite and formed of different perspectives), on the other, the "empirical receiver." While the first is a "constant"— as a textual "function"—the second is a "variable" to be placed *beside* the other.

In addition, the empirical receiver—just because s/he is found *beside* the internal addressee—is a subject who *does not receive the message directly*, but watches its unfolding as a "spectator." S/he is present, at a communicative process that unrolls before one's eyes as spectacle. Roland Barthes has spoken of "voyeurism" and Northrop Frye has justly written that the receiver of the literary work is an "eavesdropper," a kind of surreptitious listener, who overhears, and makes his own, a word that is not immediately and nominally directed to him. The author, well aware of this state of affairs, institutes a particular message in conformity with his/her knowledge.

On the basis of these observations, it seems impossible to doubt the reliability of Eberle's anthropological thesis, which states that theater demonstrates the schematic situation of *one character who speaks to another in front of one or more persons who listen; the invariable consists in the characters who speak, the variable in the people who listen.*

2.9. Before some recent sociological investigations took place, the role of the receiver of literary texts had been undeservedly excluded from theoretical reflections. Today we read in sociological studies of literature that "whoever wishes to know what a book is must know, first, how it has been read" (Escarpit, 1958, 113). A history of literature from the point of view of the reader has also been suggested (Jauss, 1967). Undoubtedly, the literary text does not exist outside its reception (including the first reading by the author): it exists only as the physical matrix of a series of variable moral experiences in which its reality is constituted. Therefore, it is not incorrect to say that *a text is the sum of its readings*, with the implicit ideal of a "history" of reading, which would consider successive periods, and therefore successive cultures and tastes.

2.10. To affirm that a text equals its reception is to refer to diverse interpretations, and also to intimate and very private responses. If someone were to write, as Jauss proposes, a history of literature from the user's point of view, it would be necessary to establish a typology of empirical readers to compare their readings with those of prefigured readers in each cultural area.

The latter readings result from the text's internal orientations and from the philological and historical reconstructions that the text must confirm. Such an effort could employ traditional research techniques of the "history of criticism" or "fortune of an author" types. However, on the personal and subjective plane, it is only recently—and amidst the innumerable difficulties that face an undertaking of this kind—that the adventure has been undertaken (Groeben, 1972; Segers, 1978). It goes without saying that documentary material with regard to the past will always be insufficient. The few and sporadic items of interest that have come down to us do not constitute a sufficient corpus. In addition, also with regard to research in possible actual documents, a notable difficulty arises, namely that of establishing what type, or better, what types of readers are to be favored. Confronted with these problems, I shall indicate—on the theoretical, and schematically typological plane—only *two* kinds of reading which, in their very abstraction, are valid for all times: (a) *ingenuous and consumistic reading*, and (b) *specialist reading*.

2.11.0. Ingenuous or consumistic reading could also be defined as "first degree," insofar as it regards not only a class of readers but constitutes the initial stage of any kind of reading, before any eventual deeper reading (which would be precisely of the "specialist" type).

The text appears, in any case, *as a complex of elements, only some of which seem to be structured*. As we shall see, the quantitative rapport between "structured" and "non-structured" parts is a variable. However, the interpretative structuration of the text is never *total*.

2.11.1. This is principally due to the fact that a "phatic" function of the literary text is possible only at the theoretical level, that is, as an ideal address, and has nothing to do with the amount of real interlocutory phaticity involved. An effective control of contact is never possible. Nevertheless, one can speak of a phaticity peculiar to literature, that constituted by the text's "spell," its "charm"—Boudoin would say its "hypnotism."

In material terms, we speak of an involving plot, of emotional implications, of anxiety deriving from uncertainty and ambiguity, of tension surrounding the motivation both of characters and action, of associative fascination, of stylistic admiration, of hallucinatory power of the rhythm, etc. And, in psychoanalytic terms, we speak of the stimulation of daydreams, the release of personal, intimate associations; we speak, in Freudian terms, of the hallucinatory realization of unconscious desires, of unloading of affective potential. We speak also of the strange phenomenon, still in part unexplained, that Coleridge defined in that brilliant formula "suspension of disbelief," that is, that singular, tacit pact stipulated between sender and receiver, by which the latter, knowing that the text is fiction, yet accepts it as truth. Octave Mannoni (1969) says that we are aware of the trick at the conscious level, but that there is something in us—perhaps our latent and never totally destructible infantile disposition—that leads us to identify trick with truth. Literature, we well know, can be profoundly moving, even to tears. In any case, then, the text "fascinates" and "involves" us; and herein lies its "phatic" function.

2.11.2. From the moment of fascination, when our attention is arrested, begins the textual adventure or the "textual voyage," as Maria Corti would say. Jan Mukařovský (1966; 1973; 149–188) has propounded the question in these terms: There are two attitudes to take in confronting the work, and they are both present in every act of reception. One is turned toward the work's "semiotic" values (strictly speaking, these compose an "intentional" communication); the other "lives" the work directly as reality (in which case, the work appears not as "sign" but as "thing"). To explore the text as "thing" or "object" is to bring out an intentionality which is a product of the rapport between reader and the text's component parts, and which the reader structures as though they were intentional. Even Francesco De Sanctis, after having made the distinction between the "intentional world and the effective world, what the poet wanted, what the poet produced," declared that in sum "the safest method is to look at the book in itself, and not in the author's intention."

Obviously it is not always possible to establish, with certainty, what the author did or did not intend. In fact, all those parts that are opposed to the textual unity constructed by the reader seem to him/her to be unintentional *because* they disturb that unity as s/he sees it. Recent semiotics has clarified the problem. We read, for example, in Eco's *Theory of Semiotics* (1976a, 261–276) that the literary text comes together on three levels, one "codified"— corresponding to Mukařovský's "intentionality"— one "overcoded," and one "undercoded." The second level is constituted by the zone, generally called "connotative," in which a second signification is made possible by a prior signification; sense unfolds by means of a successive coordination of the text's components, an "ulterior" sense contained neither "in one or in the sum of the component parts" (Mukařovský, 158). The third level constitutes the text's simple "materiality" where there are no "signs," but, if anything, "stimuli" (Eco, ibid., 19–20). Margins of these material residues, sometimes considerable, always remain in the work in sufficient quantity to exceed the interpretative model. These constitute what is normally called— adopting a scientific concept—"entropy," but I have defined the process elsewhere as "waste" with regard to hermeneutic modelization (Pagnini, 1970).

2.11.3. The ingenuous or mass reader—or, if neither ingenuous nor mass, then the first-degree reader—comes to a halt fairly soon on the long, never-ending road of interpretation. With regard to works that contain a factual narration, such a reader finds a sufficiently structured story which is easily understandable, even if, as often happens, the "plot," that is, the order in which the text effectively presents events along the thread of narrative time, differs from the logical and chronological ("fabula") order, which results from mental recomposition. S/he also finds the structure evident, that is, the network of relationships among the various characters and, particularly in narrative (less so in the lyric), the relationship among surroundings, objects, and the characters' interiority, or the relationship of the lyric voice to the real states that the work directly imitates or to which it metaphorically refers. If, then, the work does not imitate the real, and does not refer to the real, the reader finds a ready orientation in the world of possible fantasies, though these might deform the world and use its data arbitrarily. S/he succeeds fairly easily in making out blocks of sense (thus finding him/herself already in the sphere where undercodings can be recognized), by using the guidelines supplied by titles or by particular signals distributed throughout the text (Sartre spoke of "pickets" purposely distributed here and there by the author), when there is no question of open authorial intervention, thus hypothesizing what the *Textlinguistik* theoreticians, concerned as they are with transphrastic coherence, call "deep structures." These are later integrated into a profound structure which contains the total sense (Van Dijk, 1972a; 1976, 230). The reader arrives, finally, at the more flexible levels of overcoding, applying to the text the spontaneous systems of his/her own culture which may be the same used by the author in the work of textual codification or other systems stemming from diverse cultures not present at the original codification. It has been said that in "mass" reception, a strong deformation of the message may occur because of arbitrary and aberrant applications.

Overall interpretation—either at this stage of the reading or at that of greater subtlety—produces the satisfaction of *projecting a text within the text.* One knows that words possess complex series of semic nuclei from among which the interpreter makes some selections on the basis of interpretative directives, and that the interpretation is constituted by a structure of "interpretants"— to use Charles Sanders Peirce's very useful concept—be they of a purely mental order or elaborated in writing.

The reader at the most elementary level of enjoyment receives an undoubtedly intense aesthetic gratification upon the first impact with the work. Spontaneously acquired, this initial gratification is certainly the most painless. The final deliberations upon the text comprise analyses, controls, comparisons, judgments, and corrections of one's own initial responses, all of which constitute a notable effort, although such work produces other aesthetic gratifications of greater intensity and refinement. We allow ourselves here to use the term "aesthetic" in its most generic and wide sense, to refer, that is, to a series of emotional and imaginative responses to textual stimulations. Obviously, it is not only the author who is capable of sensibility. S/he is distinguished simply by the fact that s/he *knows how* to express what is possible for everyone to feel. S/he knows how to create forms that "illuminate" what in fact already exists, in the latent or nebulous state, in ordinary feeling. Therefore—as Hugh D. Duncan has observed (1953, 5)—readers do not limit themselves simply to contemplating or to perceiving the author's emotions, but they discover how to express their own emotions through the text's words, as if those words were their own. In brief, literary texts allow their receivers to give form to their amorphous and latent feelings.

And the spontaneous kinesthetic reaction (empathetic) is also, obviously, an emotive activity. The reader is always brought to identify with the character; with the same lyric or narrative "I," and to live in it, and with it, its states of mind and the events of its fictional life. The true protagonist of the literary work is the reader. Mukařovský writes:

> In art the most fundamental subject is not the author but he to whom the work is addressed, the perceiver (enjoyer); the artist, too, inasmuch as he assumes before his own work the attitude of one who observes a work of art (and not that of one who produces it), sees and values it as enjoyer (1966; 1973, 154).

Everything happens within the sensitive and cognitive apparatus of a unique subject. The work is the field of a continuous process of "autoidentification." The author is induced—through the bonds of alterity—to identify with his/her addressee. The reader is induced to identify with the sender. Identification even takes place during the most specifically aesthetic moment—that is, in the contemplation of "adequacy of form" in its significative process, contemplation that brings—as Ernst Kris has indicated (1952, 56–63)—the ideal reliving, or imitation, of the artist's expressive process. Thus, one who receives the word "re-creates" and "creates" the work with its author.

Another kind of formal contemplation—it too a source of aesthetic pleasure—is the perception of the text's "form" in the Gestaltian sense; and that is the contemplation of the satisfying arrangement of the component parts: the so-called "good form." As the most recent reflections on textual entropy have specified (Arnheim, 1971), this satisfaction is not tied only to recurrent symmetry that, in the long run, may even lead to the immobility of sense, and so provoke boredom and indifference, but to the organic, that is, the structural dynamics of the text. In sum, I am speaking, in substance, of the aesthetic pleasure deriving from recognition of "functional coherence" which, as we shall see, is of fundamental importance with reference to the specialist level.

The receiver enjoys another kind of aesthetic response in the elementary activity of recognizing the objects therein contained; that is, in the mental process of putting the object presented in the text in relation with the "mnemistic traces" that identify it. With regard to the rapport between the world within and the world outside the work (which we discuss in depth below), this act of relating establishes the work's rapport with the states of the world. Such an evocation of mnemistic traces can also be seen as a process of "materialization" of the word, which presents itself, in part, as an empty space to be filled. This is an aspect of the aesthetic experience underlined by Roman Ingarden (1960, 86, et seq.), who spoke of words as of "potential things" that the reader "realizes." Naturally, we are talking about a phenomenon which is not only aesthetic, since it is also a characteristic of the ordinary word; however, in the reception of the literary text such activity has a particular function due to the extremely high degree of the work's evocativeness beyond the natural and ordinary referential activity of common language.

Recall our reference to Gottlob Frege's *Vorstellung*; it is specifically the receiver's memory which contributes to the schematic nature of the word. Ingarden offers the example of someone who by chance reads about an event that takes place in the streets of Paris. If s/he has never seen Paris, s/he will still experience the event by searching the memory for other plausible and adaptable urban scenes. If instead s/he has seen Paris, s/he will recur to other predeterminations, that will be, in that case, exactly respondent to reality. This phenomenon is responsible for at least a part of the variable response to the text.

There is no doubt that the artistic function of "mirroring" is important, even when the usual terms of the rapport between the work's internal and extratextual structures have to be revised, let us say, in light of Lotman's thought, according to whom the work does mirror the real, but also contributes a "model" of the real, precisely by reason of its structure.

Another integrative activity performed by the receiver is the work of filling in the spaces that the author has purposely left in the text, for which reason it is characteristically "intermittent" and "undetermined." Wolfgang Iser (1970) has spoken of the "empty spaces" left in the narrative (*Leerstellen*) as opportunities for readers actively to intervene.

In addition, we must remember that suggestivity, either in the field of image or of sensation and feeling, is never univocal. The material which gathers about a verbal stimulus is, in reality, a concurrence of associative elements, a complex of images, sensations, feelings, and memories (see James Deese, 1965). Naturally, only some of these elements will come to be considered pertinent, but the refused elements, too, have their function insofar as they are effectively present as potential components of the evocative process; and even of themselves—in their function as simple mechanism—they constitute a substantial phenomenon of the aesthetic response. In a certain kind of literature and especially in that of the *symbolist* type, the elocution is conceived in such a way as to favor a plural response, thereby fixing, at least in good part, the limits of pertinence in the spontaneously recalled associative area and pushing the ever-present phenomenon of mnesic polarization and ambiguity to the maximum.

I want to speak, finally, of aesthetic gratification—still fundamentally tied to the processes of identification—that accompanies the ideal realization of unconscious desires. There is by now a copious literature on the subject, which can be substantially epitomized in the formula that the aesthetic covering—semiotically tied to the "doubling" or "introjections" which take place in both transmission and reception—allows identifications and thoughts normally forbidden by psychic and social censure. At the end of the text, an abyss opens into the unconscious.

2.11.4. On the basis of the argument we have pursued thus far, a fundamental axiom, now universally recognized, can be stated: *the receiver of the aesthetic message is never passive.* Understanding is not an exclusively "reproductive," but also "productive" behavior, and thus does not consist only in the classic consequentiality of the direct rapport between stimulus and response. Jurij Lotman has clearly summarized the theme of message appropriation with these words (worth quoting extensively):

> The act of communication (in every case communication of a certain complexity and thus exactly relevant from the cultural point of view) is considered not as a simple transfer of the message from the sender's to the addressee's awareness without consequences with regard to its self-sufficiency but as the *translation* of a certain text from the language of my "I" to the language of your "you." The possibility of such translation depends upon the fact that the codes shared by the participants to the communication, although not identical, form a complex of reciprocally intersecting elements. But, since in the act of translation a particular part of the message is always lost, and the "I" is transformed in the "you" translation code, we lose exactly what characterizes the sender's will in its specificity, which, on the unitary plane, constitutes the most important element of the message itself. A "conflictual game" is thus created, in the course of which each individual, in taking from the counterpart, tends to reconstruct the semiotic universe according to personal

models while simultaneously maintaining an interest in conserving the speaker's particularity (1977, 10).

If this "work" performed by the addressee takes place during the normal and quotidian reception of verbal communication, it is understandable that with respect to literature it assumes wide and variously articulated dimensions, for, as we have said, literary work is very complex, decontextualized, oblique: it takes place *in absentia* from the real sender, and thus cannot be verified by the receiver. In conclusion, we can repeat, with Paul Valéry, that "a creator is one who makes others create."

The reader's normal anticipation in and of itself constitutes an "active," if indirect, fact. The author, in his/her behavior as other, keeps this in mind, as we have seen, with the aim of ratifying, opposing, or modifying it. S/he knows, for example, that the reader usually expects the work to produce a "truth," a "value," something that, directly or indirectly, expresses a teaching, provokes a "coming to consciousness." S/he knows that the reader expects a logical procession of the causal chains (especially in the novel and in the theater), a conformity to "genres" (a lyric that begins as "sonnet" must end as such), a stylistic congruence (which, obviously, also includes the rules of polystylism), a tonal uniformity, and so on. Or, in periods of innovative ferment, such as ours, s/he knows that it has become normal to anticipate sudden subversion of normal expectation. In any case, the author plays upon the intentionality that the reader projects, actively, into the text; and from this dialectic between two intentionalities, sometimes opposed, the "sense" of the discourse ensues.

2.11.5. In conclusion, one who has "received" has also "collaborated" in the work. The work has "enriched" the receiver's sensibility and knowledge, has provided an awareness of certain states of the world, and insight into interior states of being, but the receiver has also "enriched" the text by pouring into it his or her own feelings and insights. S/he has been "interpreted," but has also "interpreted" and has interpreted him/herself. S/he has received a new vision of things (Corti says that "the poetic text emits a message that changes the grammar of vision of its readers in the face of reality" [1978c, 80], but has also made the text function in a way which the author might never have thought possible).

2.12.0. We turn next to "specialist" reading. As we have seen, reception of the literary message always consists in a kind of *textual reelaboration*. The text is an object of knowledge, and knowledge implies, in any case, a "transformation" (cf. Casetti, 1977, 151). In first-degree reading, such work is spontaneous enough, since the receiver, limiting him/herself to a superficial decodification, uses interpretative systems that constitute an immediate store of cultural knowledge. In general, the reader employs interpretive habits acquired during a normal education and consolidated through a practical application that does not involve profound and complex problematics. Usually the aesthetic pleasure that s/he derives from ordinary reading habits is satisfying. If it were not, it would be necessary to acquire non-immediate interpretative systems, an often tiring chore. The typical "bourgeois" refuses this effort, may even declare it maddening and useless, and tends to wrench free from the book by replacing it with an easy consolatory structure of interpretants. But if curiosity or dissatisfaction due to the text's greater resistance to the application of immediately available codes pushes this reader to a more precise and articulated knowledge, s/he will turn to "criticism" for help, that is, to the activity of specialists who have explored the text in a more selective and comprehensive manner. Such additional information offers not only the findings of more adventurous exploration to determine greater perspectives on the ground of materiality, but corrects possible aberrant interpretations, and brings what may have been blurred impressions into focus.

The "specialist" reader is, in substance, one who has a greater knowledge of the work's structural complexity, who is more conscious than the ordinary reader of the malaise that underlies the fundamental ambiguity of the aesthetic text, who is not happy with over-simplifications and reductive readings, who has at his/her disposal greater complexity of cultural systems to be applied and recognized, not least, those offered by a rigorous philological reconstruction of the linguistic ambience and a precise re-evocation of the cultural space in which the work was conceived.

To this kind of observer the text appears as *a large structured complexity*, in which s/he recognizes *multiple "levels"* (and "isotopies"[3]) structured both on their *own planes and in an interplanary sense*. It appears, that is, as a complex which is polistructured both *horizontally* and *vertically* (Pagnini, 1974).

2.12.1. In detail, the specialist reader follows the practices listed below:

a) *Recognizes in the text the "system" or "systems" to which the text leads, and verifies if, and how, each such system has been respected or violated.*

We have seen that innovative work violates one or more of its systems. In the violation of the code's rules, Umberto Eco has directly recognized the literary text's "ambiguity" and the foundation of its aestheticity. He says that ambiguity "functions as a sort of introduction to the aesthetic experience; when, instead of producing pure disorder," it attracts the addressee's attention, to urge him/her to an "interpretive effort" (1976a, 263). It is usually verifiable that a violation worked on a level of "expression" brings—as I have already indicated—a new expressivity on the plane of "content."

It is not to be believed, however, that even the most innovative work contests *all* the systems which refer to its multilevelled complexity. In general, it respects *some systems*, and these function to insure contact with the addressee. (In such cases, the reading is grafted upon what the reader is able to recognize without too great an effort.) Even the most revolutionary text *respects and violates* at the same time.

I have said, however, and it is useful to repeat—that there is also a kind of literature that *does not contest any system*, but need not for this reason be classified among second-rate products. A preoccupation of our time is that of evaluating the literary product only on the basis of its violent "refusals," a predilection consecrated in the formalist concept of "estrangement." Literature that "repeats" can be a tired product, mass-produced, kitsch; it can, however, have a special value. In Neoclassical culture, for instance, in which the principle of "imitation" dominates, the major works are *within*, not *against* systems. Alexander Pope was to catch the literary ideal of his time in the formula "What oft was thought, but ne'er so well expressed." The history of literature demonstrates the existence of strong currents of thought given over to perfecting certain systems. A comprehensive study, let us say, of the English theater in the time of Elizabeth and James I would indicate the "maturation" (the term frequently used in literary history where the organic-biological metaphor prevails) of certain formal practices: blank verse moves from its initial rigidity to a perfect flexibility and expressivity; the mounting of double or multiple plots moves from purely practical and material combinations to a closed structuration complete with complex interactions and mirrorings. Or it would be enough to look at phenomena of collective style such as Petrarchism, to have a picture of fixed systems, even stereotypes, which, however, may be open to brilliant "variations" (along with possible deterioration and passive repetition).

b) *Projects into the text a system of his/her own competence, and sees whether that system functions as a "model."*

I said "projects," not "recognizes." We are talking about an operation that is usually, though not necessarily, carried out some time after a work appears. The receiver invests the text with his/her own culture and feelings. Umberto Eco has illustrated this process very well, and it is worthwhile citing his entire description:

> The reading unfolds . . . in continuous oscillation, in which one moves from the work to the discovery of original, and therefore suggestive, codes, then to an attempt to construct a reading faithful to the work; from this point, one returns again to today's codes and lexicons to try them on the message; then one goes on to the continuous work of comparing and integrating the various reading

keys, enjoying the work also for the ambiguity that does not arise
only from the informative use of signifieds with respect to the original code, but from the informative use of signifiers as conductors
to our arrival codes (1968, 98).[4]

One might observe, in addition, that not all the grids that we
apply to literature are *given* systems, given, that is, by the culture
which produced the work and/or the culture to which we belong.
There is a procedure by which the interpreter

c) *Constructs "models" by means of inferential processes.*

S/he applies "internal" rules, taken from (a) the *corpus* of the
entire production of the author under examination—the rules
of the "macrotext," and/or (b) the single work under examination—the rules of the "microtext."

In the first case, the cognitive system—or systems, if the macrotext is not considered as an homogeneous whole, but is sub-
divided into "groups" of homogeneous components—is used *like*
a code to be projected (and recognized) in the microtext, which
turns out to be *like* the actualization of the said systems. In substance, the interpreter extrapolates a kind of "regular practice"
from within a writer's activity. In the second case, the single text
offers to the observer the laws of its own idiolect, which, once
revealed, are used *as if* they were a code upon which the text
has founded its own actualization.

I've said, "*as if they were a code.*" In reality this state of affairs
must be clarified. The idiolectic system of an author is not the
same thing as cultural systems, which pre-exist the composition
of the work. The internal system of which we are speaking is (a)
autoproduced by the *corpus* of the author, and (b) does not always
pre-exist in that corpus (considered diachronically) the composition of the single work under examination. It may be that preceding microtexts have been forming a system to which the
author remains consciously or unconsciously faithful, but it may
as well be the case that systematic clarity comes about by means
of compositions to come which would then throw a retrospective
light on the expressive venture that they were constructing, with

greater or lesser clarity and deliberation, that venture which was to become the idiolect of the macrotext.

This distinction, as we know, may apply also to non-idiolectic, that is collective, cultural systems. We have already had occasion to observe that authors compose texts without always applying norms clearly acquired from tradition, but achieving a systematicity as they work, proceeding according to intuition and instinct. The distinction is useful because it allows us to get away from the presupposition that any artistic activity may be considered a "conditioned," and in the final analysis, passive operation. We said in the preceding section that in the artist's activity we can observe more than actualization processes (even though these may be highly creative) or the original mounting of heterogeneous systems, or—and this is obvious—the formation of idiolects. We may also see his/her participation, or collaboration, in the formation of systems that only later come to be recognized as such, and projected retrospectively. This activity takes place not only in the relationships that an author establishes with a culture, but also in those that s/he establishes with his or her own inner world, and thus with the arc of production itself.

As a final possibility, in our listing of the interpreter's activity, let us now consider the case in which the reader

d) *Identifies a materiality of the text that s/he cannot insert in any "given system" and cannot interpret by means of any "model."*

In such a case, the materiality remains inert, or the reader responds to "stimuli" freely and privately. In the second case, responses are too confused to be systematized and often too profound to be objectified. We know that there is a kind of literature that points programmatically to this effect. "Sugerer, voilà le rêve!" Mallarmé used to say.

Having said this, we come to the last operation performed by the specialist interpreter of the literary text. After the above-indicated activity s/he will be confronted with a multiplicity of levels constituted by physical-technical structuration, by historical reconstructions of cultural systems, and by a-historical projections of other systems that are nevertheless supported by the text. Such multiplicity will appear to evidence no, or only partial, relationships and will constitute in its complexity a kind of new entropy, arising also from the fact that at each semantic and formal level, final structurations can be recognized on the basis of the principle of "isotopies."

Once the text has been perceived as a great complex of recognized but as yet unrelated structurizations, it is necessary to

e) *Construct, in the multiplicity of levels of structuration, a "hermeneutic model" (through fundamentally "vertical" operations).*

This "model" is actuated by means of a newly attributed pertinence in the data collected, this time all together, independently from their single coherences. A unitary vision will emerge that pacifies—in large part at least—the malaise that the text's receiver feels before its entropy. The text becomes, in fact, a global cognitive possession.

But it is not a question—one must insist—of *absolute* possession, because the hermeneutic pertinence achieved carries some "refusals" itself: something that is not specified remains at the margins of the "model," and therefore returns to "materiality." This means that it may be reopened as an unexplored horizon, alluring, troubling. The "hermeneutic model" pacifies the interpreter only in part. S/he knows, however, that consolation is temporary. The text *promises to say*, and in fact always *will say*, more than the hermeneut from time to time allows.

What the "hermeneutic model" does not specify (or wastes) remains available, together with all the other formants returned to zero degree, for another "hermeneutic model" which, practicing a different kind of specification, claims certain materiality for sense (the "symbol" becomes "sign") and leaves other elements in the material state.

The activity I am talking about—hermeneutic interpretation—unfolds in two directions: horizontal and vertical. That is, it not only uses different levels of structurations, but puts them into interdependent and interfunctional relationships. Thus the text will appear to have a compactness that did not result from the analysis of its levels. And the "motivation" of its constituents will also emerge. In such a way the literary text will be distinguished from the non-literary (the text of practical communication) because its signifiers tend to *be the most highly motivated* with regard to the signified, exactly contrary to Ferdinand de Saussure's definition of the signifier/signified rapport in ordinary language, which he defined as "arbitrary."

Some objections have been raised to the Saussurian thesis. Emile Benveniste, for one, affirms that the "bond between signifier and signified is not arbitrary; on the contrary, it is *necessary*. . . . The two are impressed together in my spirit; they reawaken *together* in every circumstance" (1939).[5] But non-arbitrariness (or the strong tendency towards non-arbitrariness) of poetry is not a question of sense "accustomed" to its vehicle—that could never be, insofar as the word of poetry is fundamentally neologistic; rather, it regards associations that are "artistically" motivated, that is, not motivated because of metonymic sedimentation. Proof of the phenomenon of the literary text's interlevel functionality lies, however, in the absolute untranslatability of the original text into other-language texts. This is precisely because its physical-technical elements are not mere vehicles of sense but unsubstitutable determinants.

The "hermeneutic model" always constitutes, then, a *partial approach*. And this is also due to the fact that it generally proceeds from *one* textual place, a level or an isotopy. Usually, one accedes to the complexity of a work, beginning with one of its planes. For example, the interpreter can begin with an analysis attentive either to the plane of expression or to that of its elements, and from that basis develop the inferences or hypotheses later to be controlled on the other planes. Or s/he can start by extrapolating a model of one of the structures forming the plane of content, and then find a convalidation from among the diverse elements on the plane of expression. At this point, a structural prospect opens upon the entire text in accordance with one of its "hermeneutic modelizations," *from a privileged point of view*. At one time, one proceeded principally from the plane of content, not bothering too much about control of forms, almost as though forms were just simply passive and inert vehicles of sense, as they are in the practical communication of language ("practical" not "emotive," since in the latter the signifier—as Charles Bally [1932] has already magisterially shown—has clear connotative functions). Today the conviction is sufficiently widespread—thanks first to stylistics and then to formalism and structuralism—that the nature of the signifier has its own decisive function in the determination of sense.

For this reason, as Gianfranco Contini suggested in one of his often cited metaphors, it is advisable, though starting from a partial point of view, to aim at the totality of the work: "However judicious and limited the procedure may be, the final aim of any discourse on any author is to lay bare the integrity of this author; lighted by a single reflector, flattened into a single point, with its emphatic dissymmetry of light and shadow, the complete author must nevertheless be caught" (1951; 1970, 169). I have already observed that this totality can never be completely encompassed, but even so the specialist interpreter *must try to cover as much as possible*. In fact, if the "hermeneutic model" leaves too much textual space unused, the excessive partiality of the approach will be revealed as a defect in the hermeneutic activity itself.

I am convinced that the critical method, issuing from formalism and structuralism, and now merged into a kind of practice that merits the adjective "semiotic" ("semiotic criticism")—especially if this is applied, as I try to suggest here, with an exact knowledge of the literary text's pragmatic reality—can be satisfactorily inclusive of the most important procedures until now separately followed.

It is perhaps useful to specify that "semiotic" and "criticism" ("criticism" as "hermeneutic modelization") are not two identical activities (see Casetti, 1977, 146–155), the one being a theory that studies the systems of signifiers and the mechanisms of signification, the other being an interpretative practice. But the label "semiotic criticism," however, is appropriate for an activity that founds its knowledge of how the aesthetic message functions upon the theoretical teachings of textual semiotics. However, the same distinction between theory and practice, with its specific finalities, was also found in the appellative "structural criticism," and it will always be in every label that indicates the science, or, in any case the discipline, that critical activity takes as a basis. It is clear as well that "semiotic criticism," simply by virtue of its particular teleology, is not a "surpassing" of structuralism, but rather an enlargement of its confines, initially limited to consideration of the text solely as "object." In reality, the conspicuous organization of the parts making up the textual complexity and their final organization in the "hermeneutic model" does not surpass, but rather confirms the principle that the text is a "structured complexity"—or, to be more accurate, a "structured and indefinitely structurable complexity."

2.12.2. Such "infinity" of the text has constituted—constitutes yet—one of the basic preoccupations of our time, and is at the center of attention in the thought of Jacques Lacan, Jacques Derrida, and the Tel Quel group (in particular Philippe Sollers, Julia Kristeva, and Roland Barthes). According to the psychoanalytic linguistics of Lacan, the sense of language flees *ad infinitum* under the signifier, as perpetual manifestation of a subject conceived as an irresolvable metonymy of itself. One understands that in transferring such a conception of being—or "lack of being"—from the sphere of psychoanalysis to that of textual analysis, the literary text itself comes to consist in a perpetual generation of free signifieds, especially if not only lexemes, syntagms and phrases are made to contribute to the structuration of sense but also their fragmentation into minimal units, such as the syllable, or even the phoneme (as in the practice of "anagrammatic" criticism[6]).

A similar linguistic conception reveals the ideology of "absence" (Barilli, 1974), to which we have already referred. The subject is annulled in the text, being only an effect of language, being *thought* by the "signifying chain" and thus constituted by the founding laws of language (metaphor, metonymy). But the text also constitutes itself as *absence of the object.* The signifier—

true absolute despot, and only survivor in this spectral reign—
has "assassinated" (says Lacan) the "thing" (absent) and assumes
ghostly meanings, elusive and delusory, regressing perpetually
toward unreachable desire.

One understands that a conception of this kind, applied to the
reading of the literary text, cannot do otherwise than reveal in
itself congeries of signifying chains, with continuous generation
of signifieds—of metaphor upon metaphor, of metonymy upon
metonymy, of paronomasia upon paronomasia. The last phase
of Roland Barthes' thought and practice reveals the influence
of such doctrine. This scholar's recent definition of "text" is
worth rereading:

> *Text* means *tissue*; but where until now one has always understood
> this tissue to be a product, an already made veil behind which, more
> or less hidden, is the sense (the truth), now we accentuate, in the
> tissue, the *generative idea* by which the text makes itself, works by
> means of a perpetual texturing; lost in this tissue—this texture—
> *the subject unmakes itself there*, like a spider that would dissolve itself
> by itself in the constitutive secretions of its web (1973, 100–101).[7]

Since things have gone so far, this seems an opportune moment to distinguish between "infinity" of the text as an interpretative variable (because of the application of diverse systems,
and of the dialectic of two subjects, the one that sends the message, the other that receives it, which takes place over the whole
range of introjective doublings of the sender and of the addressee, that constitutes the phenomenology of the text pragma-
linguistically understood), and "infinity" as one reality void of
sending subject and referential object, in which the receiving
subject as well becomes annulled in the vortical laws of language.
These two conceptions are not to be confounded, the second
coming into being under the insignia of irrationality, while the
first is pledged to a rational view of communicative facts in their
historical reality, a reality that consists both in the effort of the
philological recognition of the initial communicative process and

in the mechanism of its irrefutable transformation in diverse historical spheres and in its impact upon diverse personalities.

2.12.3. Turning now to the initial presentation of our discourse, that is, to a theory of the application of systems to the literary text, it is the systematic procedures of "criticism" which remain to be considered.

To practice literary criticism means to reduplicate the text with another text by means of metalinguistic operations (constantly referential) according to "behavioral models" founded upon (a) ideology, (b) philosophy, (c) aesthetic conceptions, (d) critical "genres" (specific lexicons, dianoetic procedures, etc.), and (e) scientific knowledge. What we call "method" is no more than the constant and coherent application of systems that are in large part preconstituted.

2.12.4. We list, then, in condensed form, the "procedural systems" most frequently used in criticism, leaving aside the procedures of "textual criticism," where it may be necessary to "fix" the text, and also of criticism as "integration" into or "comment" upon the text, meant to fill the spaces left in the writing (since, as we have seen, the text never says everything, and its underlying intentions always relate to the prefiguration of the implicit addressee, whose competence the real receiver may lack). The list will necessarily be *typological*; but we know that various reading procedures do not necessarily single out only *one* approach from among the variety of available types. It usually happens that, even in the reading methods most easily "labeled," collateral methods are applied along with the privileged one. In fact, more and more frequently now, we are implementing the kind of approach that brings a conspicuous number of systems into effect in direct rapport with our knowledge that the artistic text is many-sided. Criticism is a multiple genre, availing itself of a variety of disciplines that our culture generously offers and that it is not possible to ignore. And semiotics, the total science of communication, appears to be the discipline most suited to become a doctrinal basis for multiple operations. Further, it also offers the advantage—not to be overlooked—of a reception of the literary fact with no, or with very few, prejudices of an ideological order.

a) Judge the work. This means to evaluate it on the basis of preestablished normative systems (abstracted or demonstrable in model works), exalting its conformity, and holding it therefore "correct," "satisfactory," "beautiful," and so on, or indicating its "errors," and in practice, proposing a "correct" text to replace the "incorrect" one (*evaluative criticism*).

The judgment of value is always a comparative assertion (comparison with other works, comparison with the idea of beautiful work), and therefore always deductive. A reading without presuppositions does not exist (even if the reading modifies the critic's nomological assumptions, predisposing him/her, thus, to make new evaluations).

The evaluation does not take place, usually, with a simple axiological assertion, but with a series of examples and clarifications, which, however, do not have *demonstrative* value of the judgment's "truth"—truth that, in principle, cannot be demonstrated; if anything, these examples function to support the procedure's coherence or to attract the reader to the qualities and aspects of the work that the critic has appreciated (or not).

R. T. Segers (1978, 8–88) indicates some of the major literary norms:

i) *Literature as "imitation" of the states of the world* (the eighteenth-century poetics of Nature "description" for example, or the Marxist theory of "mirroring" the social situation).

ii) *Literature as "fantasy."* Literary signs need not refer to states of the world but to fantasies.

iii) *Literature as linguistic "écart"* (the Russian formalist theory of "estrangement").

iv) *Literature as "contestation" of ruling socio-cultural systems* (poetics of the *avant-garde*).

v) *Literature as "complexity."* The work must be able to be variously interpreted.

vi) *Literature as "structural unity."* The work must be compact, economically constructed with interrelated parts.

vii) *Literature as "epochal survival."* The work's greatness is measured by its ability always to respond to the demands made upon it by the various epochs in which it is received.

The list can go on (Segers himself declares that it is not exhaustive). Let us add

viii) *Literature as "transparency of sense"* (the poetics of Classicism).

ix) *Literature as "imitation of the classics"* (the poetics of the Renaissance and of Classicism).

x) *Literature as "opacity"* (the poetics of Symbolism).

xi) *Literature as "sentiment"* (the poetics of Romanticism).

xii) *Literature as "political commitment,"* etc.

b) Compare the text with other texts by the same author or by different authors in order to reveal its peculiarities. This process determines affinities and contrasts (*comparative criticism*). It can also establish "values" (*evaluative criticism*).

c) Relate textual elements to occurrences and motives in the author's life (*biographical criticism*). If the author is understood as psychological individuality, Freudian criticism results, the type conducted by Freud himself and later by some of his students (*biographical-psychoanalytic criticism*).

d) Consider an author's *opera omnia*, or suitable regroupments of works in the arc of an author's production as "texts" ("macrotexts") and analyze them as such. The "macrotext" will then serve to illuminate and enrich every single component ("microtext") (*macrotextual criticism*).

Because of its practicality, "macrotextual" criticism is the most widely adopted. But strictly speaking, the only mode to which one cannot take exception is the "micro-macrotextual" reading. This consists of the in-depth reading of a single work with the help and in the sense of the macrotext, or some macrotexts. In such a way the practice is not reductive but respectful of the single structure, and does not preclude—to follow the logic of the macrotext, which is, in practice, a statistical logic—evaluation of the *hapax legomenon*.[8]

e) Specify the language of the work by means of an attentive reconstruction of the linguistic sphere in which the work was written (*philological criticism*).[9]

f) Beginning with the concept that the literary work gives form to the author's feelings in an autonomous and unrepeatable mode, investigate and characterize its lyrical-sentimental moment (*idealistic criticism*).[10]

g) Presupposing that the work reflects and is determined by a set of ideological convictions, of artistic conceptions, or feelings that the writer has drawn from the cultural *humus* of his time and has elaborated, reconstruct this set in order to explain the forms and contents of his/her product (*historicistic criticism*).[11]

h) Presupposing that the mark of poetic language is constituted by the "emotive" use of language, study the linguistic "digressions" that emotivity has produced in comparison with the norm (*stylistic criticism*).[12]

i) Presupposing, on the basis of Marxist theories, that the economic-social situation produces a determined dominating class, an ideology and its intellectuals, and then too the writer and his/her ideas, taste, style, and even connivances and reactions, take the work back to his/her cultural milieu and reconstruct from it the learning process of the world as historically determined practice (*Marxist criticism*).[13]

j) Utilizing Marxist theories, reconstruct the dynamics of the work's production and consumption in a socially determined ambience (*sociological criticism*).[14]

k) Liberate—almost confessionally—subjective and intimate reactions to the text. Make a total identification of the critical subject with textual reality (*hermetic criticism*).[15]

l) Reveal *how* a work is structured. The work appears as a complex of levels each structured in itself and all structured as a whole (*formalistic-structuralist criticism*).[16]

m) Reconstruct the sign systems that compose a work, either as physical sets regulated by laws or as semantic systems and compare them with the literary and non-literary systems with which the text places itself in rapport. The text will emerge as a bundle of actualizations/variations/substitutions (*semiotic criticism*).[17]

n) (Re)construct the "model" that unifies the various levels of a text or of a macrotext, and perhaps interpret such a "model" in the light of contemporary cultural systems (*structuralistic-hermeneutic* and *semiotic-hermeneutic criticism*).

o) Availing oneself of the theory of "archetypes," see the work as bearer of symbols, schemes, models, all understood as reincarnations of elementary ideals presupposed as intrinsic givens of the human soul (*archetypal criticism*).[18]

p) Extrapolate the metaphoric material to compose it into patterns (*"imagery" criticism*).[19]

q) Utilizing the doctrine of the early Freud, identify in the text, or in the macrotext, the expressions of the unconscious. Elements that belong to manifest structurations are motivated by latent contents. Explain further the way in which unconscious fantasy transforms itself into conscious theme. If the inquiry is conducted on the macrotext, (re)construct the "system" of the transformational variants of single unconscious fantasies (*transformational Freudian criticism*).[20]

r) Utilizing Lacan's doctrine, explain a determined linguistic behavior by means of the tensive relationships between the "self" and the "Other" (*Lacanian criticism*).

s) Utilizing the Freudian theory of *Jokes and Their Relation to the Unconscious* and the concept of culture as repression, interpret certain levels of the text as "return of the repressed" or, to include political repression, as "return of the suppressed" (*Freudian repression-theory criticism*).[21]

t) Study attentively the phonic-syntactic-rhythmic structure of the discourse, both on its own level and in the implicative functions of the semantic-connotative levels (phonic *patterns*, phonic and syntagmatic iterations, paranomasia, onomatopoeia, etc. (*textural criticism*).[22]

u) Utilizing the principles of the linguistics of "absence" (Lacan)—according to which the discourse is not the place of the full presence of the signified and of the truth but of an original amnesis—and those of the "generative" theory of the text elaborated by the Tel Quel group—according to which the text does not "express," does not "re-produce," a preliminary sense, but "produces" it by means of infinite fragmentations, intertextual concurrences and reorganizations of the énoncé in the act of reading, itself infinite ("significance"), deconstruct the discourse down to its minimum components (phonemes) and perpetually reconstruct it, allowing all the significative possibilities to explode in every direction ("differance" criticism).[23]

2.12.5. I add two final observations that, even if fairly obvious, are necessary to completeness.

a) When we speak not of the text's first reception, of its first interpretation, but of reading after other readings handed down in writing or read aloud (conferences, lessons, etc.), we shall have finally to bear in mind that the single receiver of the work is now constituted by a "multiplicity," usually not only numerical but dialectical. Or, to be more precise, s/he is of course always a person, but a person in contact—ideally or practically—with other receivers. In such case, a communications network comes into being that constitutes a collaboration in the work of textual interpretation. Its phases—with acceptances, variations, substitutions, etc., are recorded in the history of criticism (see Groeben, 1972). But it is also what takes place in cases of literary or dramatic communication to groups of persons (texts read or acted before a listening public, a sufficiently common practice today). In such cases, a completely intersubjective communication can take place—exchange of impressions, criticism, comments, etc. But even without such a complete exchange, group reception is in any case intersubjective, if only because of the reciprocal influence exercised by simple emotional manifestations or the minimum kinestheses.

b) Literary criticism, too, is obviously a communicative practice wherein, therefore, one recognizes a "sender," a "text," and a "receiver." And then, since criticism is language, it is inscribed not only in theoretical and executory systems but also, contemporarily in "scriptural" systems, that is, in "lexicons," "syntaxes," etc. Finally, the presence of the "other"—and the *choice* of the "other"—orients the writing according to particular directives of rational communicativity in which subjective shadings which can neither be rationalized nor used in the coherent framework of the hermeneutic modelization are lost. The subjective response to the text is never absolutely identifiable with the criticism (not even in the partial recuperation attempted by the "hermetic" reading).

2.13. I conclude this discourse on reception with a reconsideration of "cultural systems." If these allow the reconstruction of the fundamental structuration of the subject of transmission (either as subject of the énonciation or as subject of the énoncé) and also reconstruction of the implicit, ideal addressee—that, as we have said, comes from the structure of the message itself and also from the same cultural systems that s/he naturally shares with the author by reason of the principle of alterity of the message, then cultural systems allow as well the reconstruction of the fundamental structuration of the heteroeval receiver. Heteroeval reception can be studied by means of a *comparison* of the structuration of the transmission with the structuration of the receiving subject, which, together with bringing historical and philological contributions into harmony with the whole, will reveal the forces that determine their particular emphases and their a-historical projections, constituted by their own existential preoccupations. In such a way too can the "fortune" of an author be documented in the historical and sociological sense.

THREE

Dramatic Literature and the Theater

3.0. Theater is not literature, and, in all strictness, one should not speak of it in a discourse such as this, which focuses upon literature as its specific object. However, since a large part of the theater belonging to our cultural tradition is committed to and handed down by means of written texts, and since these written texts are treated by literary critics as literature—although of a particular genre, that of "dramatic literature"—this seems an opportune place to clarify some points on the question of the written dramatic text and its relationship to the staged representation.

3.1. To consider the written text as "literature" is to postulate that it is *autonomous* and an *end in itself*; or, if it is not an end in itself, but a text that is waiting to be staged, that its staged representation is nothing more than a "variable," in a certain sense accessory to an "invariable," the text itself.

These two assumptions ignore the following facts: (a) The written dramatic text is destined to be transformed into spoken and acted text—which means its translation from one channel to another as the written word is given expression in voice and action; (b) it is conceived to be only one part—although in most cases a conspicuous one—of that great heterogeneous complex of information channels that constitute the scenic representation in its totality; and (c) it is this heterogeneous totality, knowledge of the written text not at all a condition of its comprehensibility, that constitutes theater as a complete and autonomous fact in itself.

3.2. All this considered, it is legitimate to recognize the written text as autonomous and an end in itself only (a) in the few cases in which the author may never have destined the text for the stage, but for the reader, even though it is in dramatic form (as happens, for example, in Goethe's *Faust* and in some other Romantic works), or (b) in those ambivalent cases in which the author may have foreseen the two functions: literary and theatrical.

Such is the case of the great English dramaturgy which flourished during the late sixteenth and early seventeenth centuries. Generally destined only for the stage, and therefore directly consigned, handwritten, to the theatrical company, at a certain point the texts began to appear in print in prized editions, beautifully and carefully reproduced (the works of Ben Jonson, for instance, which appeared in folio in 1616, and those of Shakespeare, which were posthumously published in folio in 1623). Evidently such publications were not brought out for practical reasons, that is, to fix authoritatively "signed" texts, in a period in which the copyright did not prevail, in order to prevent eventual pirated or arbitrary productions. Their authors must have aspired to free their work from the theatrical event, from a life like that of the poor player "who struts and frets his hour upon the stage and then is heard no more," to see it achieve a worthy place of its own in the land of letters, taking its place upon library shelves beside the immortal literary works. In this way, it acquired not only historical duration but, and this above all, became the object of the scrupulously close readings performed by expert scholars. (Some of George Chapman's plays are called "both a Poem and a Play"; but John Marston asserted in the preface of *Parasitaster* that dramas "are to be spoken, not read.") It is obvious that in cases such as these, one can and must speak of a "dramatic literature," but only in these, and as absolute exceptions to the rule.

The appearance of the written text in print, and in well-edited editions, understood to constitute the text, or, if you will, the authoritative pre-text, the archetype of productions to come, is tied to the institution of the "repertory," as defined (and dated: 330 B.C.) by Cesare Molinari (1978); that is, to the possession of texts by one or more companies "in expectation of any representation whatsoever." Repertory theater is distinct from the improvisatory theater, which continues even today, in which a performance is born in a single productive operation, the verbal text formed together with the non-verbal components. Clearly, this second kind of performance—historically speaking—cannot repeat itself: it constitutes a single event. Repertory implies—as, for example, in the revival of classical antique dramas—a *series* of different performances dependent upon a fixed written text, but consequentially offering fresh interpretations realized both in acting and staging. The historically prevalent practice in cultivated theater, that is, the textual reinterpretation that accompanies consecutive presentations, treats the written text as a first field of hermeneutic exercises before the actual production. Such treatment, because of the *scriptural* nature of the text itself, had— and has—much in common with literary interpretation. Thus, the conception of the production as of a kind of "interpretation" of the scriptural matrix inevitably prevails. Even the loosest, most aberrant modern realizations of traditional texts are taken as "readings." With regard to his *Romeo and Juliet*, Carmelo Bene declared that it represents a "critical essay *on* Shakespeare." The passage is worth citing extensively:

> Shakespeare and Marlowe . . . were the greatest of *poets* and as such remain the foremost exponents of English *literature*. But to put their theater on the stage today, however it is "revisited" or "rewritten," means to fall into equivocation. *A Midsummer Night's Dream, Romeo and Juliet* have been theater, and just for this reason are no longer, can no longer be so. I do not put Shakespeare on the stage—I've said so many times—nor one of my interpretations or readings *of* Shakespeare, but a critical essay *on* Shakespeare (1977, 19–20).

Carmelo Bene's is an extreme case, and among other things, the distinction that he makes between "interpretation" and "critical essay" would have to be clarified. But even for a less radical director like Peter Brook—to name only one among the many who share the same conviction—the "classics" must in any case be "revisited." Brook sustains that archaeology has never made good theater and that a director has a right to extrapolate a reading in keeping with the demands of his time.

For this reason, it is permissible, at least in theory, to distinguish two phases in the gestation of the production (improvisatory theater excepted): In the first phase, one must take paradigmatic possession of the text; in the second, one must mount the production. The first can indifferently be done by either litterateur, director, or actor: the interpretative act—finding a hermeneutic paradigm—can be applied with equal benefit to any literary writing. The second phase will require the special skills proper to theater people, and of this it will be necessary to speak in detail.

The "written text" is transformed into the "spoken text," which then becomes part of the "stage text," by which we mean the contextuality of the spoken text with the other concurrent texts: those of gesture, facial mimicry, costume, spatial dynamics of bodies, scenic space, scenographic illusions, light, color, sound, and so forth. The word "text" is then no longer used with reference to the verbal structure, but to indicate the set of the macrotextual components—structured/structurable—independently of their physical nature. The best approach to the script-stage rapport is to see the script as a particular structure originally written with a view to its transformation into a spoken and acted structure (vocal stress of the speech, direct syntactic comprehensibility in speech dynamics, potentiality for paralinguistic expressivity, capacity for insertion into the action, etc.), over and above the characteristics of dramatic language itself, which mimes natural discourse, as Alessandro Serpieri, following the categories of speech-act linguistics, has well observed in his "deictic-performative" approach (1977). Transformed into spoken and acted text, the deictic-performative structure is macrostructured in a "montage" with all the other non-verbal structures of the production.[1]

In the abstract, there is nothing different here from what also occurs—as we have seen—in the literary text, which itself results in a set of structured/structurable texts (levels, isotopies, cultural systems, etc). Julia Kristeva (1970, 67–69), in order to characterize the literary text, spoke of "intertextuality." But in the theater, this "intertextuality" is of a physical heterogeneity unknown to literature, which does use a great variety of structures, but always translates them into the single system of language. In place of what in narrative, for example, would be "description," in the theater we have "ostension."

The process of putting on a production brings with it a series of "receptions," which are transformed into "messages" (communicative/stimulative), or better, which merge into the scenic macrotext, which then constitutes the text of the "public reception." Director, actors, and technicians receive the written text (given, of course, that the text is something that "precedes" the staging process, and some mode of textuality is always precedent where there is no question of on-the-spot improvisation), and produce the "scenic macrotext" that becomes the publicly received text. The director-actor-technician trio then completes the two operations I spoke about above; but the second is a very complex one that without difficulty can be defined as "authorial," insofar as it sends its own messages and comes to be inserted in the scheme "author" which the receiver of the stage-text imagines as "internal sender." The public, in fact, has before it a "composite sender," formed of the author inasmuch as s/he has written both the words pronounced in the stage discourse and the instructions in the stage directions, through which s/he is the inductor, by means of textual implications, of the non-verbal part of the performance, and formed also of the director, actors, and technicians, inasmuch as they interpret the script and put on the production. The director is charged with producing the theatrical event in all its co-textuality; s/he must follow and guide the realization of the spoken and acted text, preside over the formation of all the production's other non-verbal texts in order to bring all the dramatic components within a *structured complexity*. In doing this, s/he often makes modifications, cuts, and integrations on the "sides" used by the various actors. Mukařovský noted the mutation of these "sides," saying that "the actors' scripts very rarely pass onto the stage without a dramatic adaptation, and the expression 'stage interpretation of the play' is usually only a euphemism that masks the tension between theater and literature" (1966; 1973, 308). In addition, the director tasks him/herself to establish an *active rapport* (this being his/her particular form of phatic contact) with the spectator, a practice of an artistic nature that consists in making sure that the audience, without excessive effort, will understand the laws of the communicative-stimulative macrostructure. As the author has already done at the moment of planning the text, the director imagines an "addressee," who, here too, will naturally be historical and contingent, but different from that of the author who may not have written for the same public (a very rare case), and establishes with it his/her other-oriented automessage.

The actor, beyond following directions, contributes to the production through a special compromise constituted by the rapport between his/her own "personality" and "role." The actor is an "I" who works within a fantasy of being a "s/he," the particular statute that permits us to distinguish the performative deictics of dramatic art—that is "simulation" (Eco, 1973b; Gullì Pugliati, 1976, 183 et seq.)—from the performative deictics of ordinary linguistic behavior in practical life. To the character outline formed in the words of the written text, or, more precisely, in the interpretation of the text's words and of the play's paradigmatics, the actor contributes his/her own concrete individual nature, made up of a certain particular sensibility, voice, body, mimicry, as well as the dynamic and physical stature of his/her own body (the plasticity of the actor has much in common with that of sculpture and dance). S/he substitutes, in brief, a complete and particular person for the character-type that emerges from the dialogue.

Director, technicians, and actors, then, *offer a text*. While interpreting the master-script, they situate certain aspects of its potentiality in the foreground and relegate others to the background. While staging the drama, they collaborate to make concrete all texts—spoken and unspoken—that constitute the production. And this text of the theatrical event, unique and irrepeatable, is then offered to the interpretation of a public which recognizes the "intentional" parts and hazards itself in the non-structured zones, intent to structure them itself. And that will accomplish—again—now an ingenuous interpretation, that follows above all the thread of the action, suffers and enjoys empathetically events and situations, identifying itself with characters, now a specialist interpretation that ventures into the hermeneutics of the co-textual complex.

The "prefiguration" of the addressee in theatrical communication is much more concrete and precise than that formed in the mind of the author of literary works. It consists of audiences that are not only historically delineated, not only culturally defined, but also *empirically present* at the enunciative act. In the theater, the characteristics of the communication model come closer to those of the ordinary communication model. The sender (in this case director, actors, and technicians) and addressee (the audience) are physically each before the other. And the rapport of otherness, for this reason, is a good deal more alive and operative than in literature. Directors know that, from performance to performance, actors "feel" the public to such an extent that their behaviors are modified on the basis of the contingent and live reception. The direction itself can be transformed in the course of a performance cycle.

Naturally, the theater manifests the *oblique reception* of the message. Moreover, as I said initially, it is in all probability the prototype of all literary expressions. Of course, this holds true as well for the monologue and the direct apostrophe to the audience, since each has a formal character. The actors send each other reciprocal messages, and the apron, or in any case the scenic space, represents the breach that allows an audience *to be present* at a closed structure of relationships. One recognizes there the objectual signicity that the theater ostensively manifests since all that one sees on the stage—together with what one feels—is "artifact" sign. Still, there exists a state of *being present* that carries a direct "response," a kind of "interlocutoriness," that the actor is aware of, perhaps on the faces or in the gestures of the people in the audience in the case of a "reading," and that s/he otherwise intuits by a kind of heightened psychic awareness and also officially receives in the symbolic forms that the classical theater allows: clapping, whistling, laughing, and a few words denoting praise or displeasure.

Finally, to bring our discussion back to "cultural systems," it remains to be said that director, actors, and technicians insert and superimpose their behaviors in and upon the systematics that the author of the play had realized on his/her own account. The director not only takes note of cultural systems that have preceded the master-script's structuration (historical and philological activity in the case of heteroeval texts, undertaken of course with reference to the available dramatic criticism), but also keeps in mind contingent cultural systems which characterize the episteme and the theatrical practice of his/her own time; and s/he carries out yet once more, as the author has done, in the limits of his/her own field, passive actualizations, transformations, or innovations. Director, actors, and technicians all behave in reference to (not necessarily, I repeat, in obedience to) a behavioral systematics either of their own time or of tradition. This does not mean—as we well understand—that they always give the public what the public may expect, on the basis of its own cultural systems, but that they also establish a tensive rapport, contesting, provoking, or imposing upon the audience. They present codified together with non-codified parts. For every aspect of the stage event, there does not always exist a structure of signifiers linked/linkable with conventional structures of signifieds. What happens in literature also happens in the theater: some part of the textual material always exceeds intentionality.

This direct rapport with the contingent public brings me to a brief reflection on the representation of theatrical works belonging to diverse and distant cultures. I certainly cannot assert that a performance is good only when it scrupulously reproduces the written text and philologically conforms to the staging and acting or representative practices of the time when it was originally produced. Such a qualifying judgment cannot be pronounced but by a certain very limited sector of the audience: historians, humanists, the erudite, and perhaps not even by all of these. Theater is spectacle that aims, by its very nature, at a strong and lively collective participation, and that often assumes a ritual character. If the director does not reach for this immediate response, the drama is reduced to a cold archaeological event, to which the public responds with indifference. This being the case, the way is clearly opened to all kinds of freedom, if one thinks of the theatrical event in terms of the contrast between the historic reality of the text and the representative practices of the time of performance. And freedom, when the theater attracts a mass audience, as is common today, can easily become license. This is a phenomenon that frequently arises now among our most enterprising directors, who moreover seem to lend themselves to the savage appropriation of the entire cultural patrimony, and in a sector of activity that more than any other makes such appropriation legitimate. The "good" theatrical event, in fact, cannot be evaluated with parameters other than those of its contingent effects.

What can be said in defense of cultural patrimony? We can simply reply, as it were, morally and didactically. The erudite director faithful to the historicity both of texts and representative practices will indulge neither his/her own fantasy nor the expectations of a contemporary public, but, aware that audiences can also be modified, will try to refine their expectations. S/he will therefore see that not only does theater go toward the public, but that the public goes toward theater, and in a direction that leads no longer to innovation, but tradition. I repeat, however, that this kind of director will not necessarily put on a *better* production, but a *type* of production. In any case, we will see that s/he has also brought out—and with absolute legitimacy—certain aspects of the play's textual potentiality, and this in conformity with contemporary existential and cultural preoccupations. It is a fact that not all historical theater is always re-representable. Certain works, raving successes in their own time, can no longer be tolerated. These perhaps will have to await a change in cultural conditions before they can again be accepted.

3.3. It is evident from what I have discussed that a semiotics of theater, or a semiotic criticism of theater cannot elect the written text as the exclusive object of scrutiny. In this sense, today's scholars are almost all unanimous. We cannot even say that because there is theater there must be the word. Mime, for example, is theater without words. There is even theater without actors, as evidenced by certain moments of scenic duration in which only objects can be seen. The lively experimentation going on in contemporary theater shows that we will never be able to speak of absolute dominants. If the object of literary semiotics is the "literary text," the object of theatrical semiotics is "the performance text."

At this point, however, enormous difficulties arise, still unresolved by semioticians of the theater. The first lies in the fact that theater is ruled by the absolute predominance of the énonciation over the énoncé. It is true that while a play is being performed a spectator can mentally construct a text composed of memorial sediments and pertinences, finally to possess, when the curtain falls on the last act, a certain cotextual, contextual idea, that is, an énoncé, but it is also true that the theatrical fact is a dynamic development that, once ended, is irrecoverable and unverifiable. It is this, its particular—we could say para-existential—nature, that clearly distinguishes theater from literature, where the text is fixed and therefore recoverable and verifiable. If the laws of the literary text require that the énoncé be set, the laws of the theater are all inherent in the enunciative effect. This bears strongly upon the phenomenon of reception, the nature of which imposes on the theatrical text a certain type of communication that rests upon the semiosic act, and invokes a different study of reception from that pertaining to literature. There is also a temporal dimension in the literary text—studied by Cesare Segre (1974)—but it is followed by a freely recontemplative activity that performance cannot allow. This is why the theater demands an intense participation, levies a heavy tax upon the spectator's emotional resources. The literary text makes a stronger appeal to contemplation than to participation, which is usually relegated to the stage of "ingenuous" reception.

The second difficulty is that for every single play there is a *multiplicity* of texts. Which performance out of all those presented should be chosen as *the* one to examine? No choice can escape the arbitrary.

The third great difficulty lies in the technical—not memorial—fixing of the stage text, which may be used as the *corpus* of the analysis. The "fixed" stage text can never be something that resembles the literary text, because it will have to be *another* text (where recourse to a multiplicity of metalanguages is necessary). And this *other* text can never offer a precise image of the stage text, if for no other reason than it is only a "translation." The possibility of obtaining a recording of all the effects of scenic macrotextuality is unthinkable, even if one were to hypothesize a kind of "score"—on the model of musical texts—that registers the effects for each one of the material communication sources (proposed, in lieu of something better, by Kowzan, 1968, and Pagnini, 1970), because these effects, even if they originate from diverse channels, in any case almost always accumulate and intersect. Without speaking, of course, of the irrecoverability of past stage texts, for which the only source of information is some fortuitous documentation, usually partial and vague. Another substantial aspect of the theatrical event is irrecoverable: The fact is that the reception of the heterogeneous bundle of information offered in performance occurs not only in a particular historical situation, but also in an "emotional climate" that is not only made up of the *subject's reception* but bears the traces of the *collective reception*. Each subject in the audience is a receiver "in contact" with other receivers, and is therefore implicated in a choral reception.

It follows that it is necessary (a) to abandon the idea that one can isolate *one* particular performance to stand for a play's text, (b) to renounce the idea that one can "transcribe" (metalinguistically) *every* semiotic effect of a performance, though these may be both actual and evident, and (c) to recognize, even when *all* the semiosic effects may be successfully reconstructed metalinguistically, that these would not constitute the spectacle.

Nothing remains then other than to anticipate either (a) a theatrical semiotics that does not take the semiosic processes of one particular performance as the object of description but describes the type of semiosic processes that makes up the ideal theatrical performance, imagined in the completeness of its functions, that is, a semiotics of the "theatrical system," comparable to the now-established semiotics of the "literary system" (see, for example, Todorov, 1967), or (b) a theatrical semiotics founded on a play's historic reception according to the possible (but always partial) reconstructions on the basis of testimony.

The construction of theater's semiotic system will have—as does the construction of literature's semiotic system—two positive aspects: (a) it will be important as theory of the phenomenon—non-normative, let us emphasize, and (b) it will be important as a possibility for a fresh and enlightened return to single and concrete phenomena. Such knowledge sensitizes the receiver to the message, and permits critical approaches of particular competence and selectivity.

But there remains the embarrassing fact that one who has not been present at the performance to which a particular commentator refers will never be able to confront the critic's response with the text that has provoked it, something that the scholar of literature can always do.

3.4. It is here, then, in the ongoing polemics against the written text—which as usual risk letting the *whole* discourse slide to the opposite slope, with absurd conjectures about those who could ever have confused the written with the performed text—

that study of the text can be vindicated, even if only in its partial importance. The text—whether it exists as written pre-text or is a recorded performance—will always constitute, for good or ill, a precious and important element of the theatrical macrotext, upon which it is possible to conduct a series of hermeneutic operations and verifications. This, one well knows, in the light of knowledge of the "theatrical system" of which I spoke above, need not be of an exclusively "literary" order but oriented toward evaluations of the very "quality" of the specific theatrical language, that can be recognized in the predisposition of the word to be recited and acted. See, for example, J. L. Styan's studies of Shakespeare's texts (1971).

Further, it is by perusing the text—whether it be the one respectful of the master-text or not, recorded on tapes and then retranscribed, or the one that exists only on tape because it was never written down, or one produced by a "live" recording of an event—that its linguistic (and paralinguistic) complexity is captured. A complexity that sometimes in the immediacy of the performance does not lend itself to a total reception. It is doubtful that we would have known *Hamlet*, as we do today, if we had received only its stage realization. It is totally probable that the ever-more frequent publication of Elizabethan and Jacobean texts came about because of the felt need to conduct minute and capillary examinations. The written text also allows, and this is obvious, an easy modelization of the action of its effective "narrative" distribution, a precise reconstruction of its segments, a tabulation of the characters' physical relationships, and so forth. Further, comparison of performance with text is not a negligible operation, because it allows an evaluation of the expressivity of the eventual "disjunctions" and "innovations" used in the stage realizations.

Finally, I see no harm in speaking—as I have done elsewhere (Pagnini 1970a), thereby exciting some discussion (for example, Ruffini, 1974, 43)—of the written text as of "deep structure," understood in a wide sense. Do not director, actors and technicians first of all read and assimilate the written text (when it exists), and assimilating it, do they not perhaps put down the projectual foundations of what then will be the operative macrotext of the representation? While I would not like to affirm that every text of the stage macrotext is inscribed in the written text, I would also be reluctant to say that the written text has not suggested something of the contextuality and, possibly of the nature of macrotextuality itself. In the "montage" of all the texts that compose the performance-text there will be reciprocal relationships that constitute reciprocal determinations, and the verbal text (transformations of the written text) will thus have had its own effect (a phenomenon very clearly spelled out by Keir Elam, 1977).[2]

3.5. Perhaps something yet remains to be added, given that we are deep within the various questions of the theatrical performance. With regard to the activity performed by the receiver, it will be enough to recall the activity discussed in Chapter II, where I spoke of literary reception, and to add to it the activity specific to the spectator at the theater.

a) In the first place, the spectator accepts the "conventions" that permit him/her to frame the spectacle as "theater." Such conventions consist, in substance, in the acceptance of the "metaphoricity" (or "symbolicity") of all that is seen on the stage. In other words, s/he not only accepts minor conventions like that of the monologue or of the aside, but also accepts the idea that all that one sees and hears at the theater is *itself and other than itself*; it is framed in a great paradigmatic of sense. It can serve to remind us of a not too paradoxical remark made by Aldous Huxley that pertained to literature, but naturally includes the theater, and that is that life never makes sense and literature always does.

b) Second, s/he makes an intense effort to make sense of the information received from the performance's many simultaneous channels, an effort aggravated by the fact that the information is inexorably tied to its dramatic duration.

c) Third, s/he establishes an ambiguous rapport with the state and particularly with character, a rapport of involvement, or of identification, through which the barriers of "pretending" fall; a relationship of detachment and contemplation, through which the "pretense" is "pretense" and is judged as "art." Character is empathetically lived—with all that this implies of profound and unconscious implications—but at the same time it is seen and heard and is praised or blamed on the basis of its level of ability.

d) Fourth, s/he contemplates and judges the interpretative and directive data on the basis of dynamic models that the performance raises little by little as it unfolds.

e) Fifth, s/he interprets the performance not only on the basis of epistemological, ideological, and other "systems" in his/her possession (on this point we refer to our observations on literary interpretation) but also on the basis of the "systems" of staging practices acquired through experience of other theatrical events.

f) Sixth, s/he compares the realizations of the performance with others of the same play that s/he has seen. And, if s/he knows the written text, evaluates the skill with which directors, actors, and technicians have interpreted and put into effect.

g) Seventh, s/he integrates, in fantasy, the stage frame using some essential suggestions of the representation (in some cases reduced to very few symbolic elements).

h) Finally—as I said above—the personal response to the performance is inevitably intermingled with the shared reception (by other persons in the audience).

FOUR

Reference

4.0. A discourse that wishes to confront the problem of literature's rapport with the world necessarily implies taking a position
with regard to the various linguistic theories on the sign-referent
rapport. Still, the position I have already taken with regard to
culture as a complex of "systems" that constitute the subject's
fundamental structures, either as world view and behavioral
norms or as confuted and negated institutions—which for this
very reason are always *present*—thereby excludes of itself certain
traditional theses.

a) It obviously excludes the Platonic position, according to
which linguistic and extralinguistic facts are connected by a fixed,
natural rapport—a transcendent rapport in which man has no
part. It is excluded because it conceives "systems" as cultural
products, destined to vary and to be substituted in time.

b) It also partially excludes the Aristotelian position, according
to which knowledge of the world preexists and is independent
of language, which does no more than fix such knowledge by
means of an arbitrary, even if conventional, rapport with things.
I have spoken, in fact, of culture preexistent to and culturally
inherited by the subject, thereby constraining the subject to structure itself within culture, to see things in conformity with its
paradigms. But I have also recognized in the subject the power
to enrich, to modify, and also to destroy systems.

c) It excludes as well the thesis held by certain linguists according to whom one must speak of a fixed bipolar rapport
between "sign" and "signified." My pragmatic discussions on the

production and reception of the sign are closer, if anything, even if not integrally, to the theses of the behaviorists: a large part of the signified is caught precisely in the "behavior" of the subject who produces and uses the sign and of the subject who responds to the sign's stimulus.

d) My position also refuses the thesis of those who postulate a direct rapport between "sign" and "referent." It accepts, rather, the proposal made by Ferdinand de Saussure, according to whom the sign does not have a direct rapport with things but establishes it through the concept ("signified"). It therefore includes the triadic rapport among "signifier" and "signified" (concept)—constitutives of the "sign"—and among "sign" and "referent." And it includes, therefore, what is established by J. Stenzel, according to whom "the significative signs of the verbal expression acquire in their turn an objectivity that stays within the knowledge of the speaker and the signified object . . . separating them . . . and nevertheless making the tie between them possible" (1934, 35). This *intermediary* "objectivity"—that J. L. Weisgerber then defined as "Zwischenwelt" (1962, 58)—is the "vision of the world" constituted by "cultural systems." For this reason we accept the principle—sustained today by many linguists—that language is not a passive mirror of reality, but, on the contrary, a structure projected upon reality and conferring upon it the forms of its entities and parts, of its relationships and its segmentations (Humboldt, Cassirer, Trier, Peirce, Morris, Wittgenstein, Hjelmslev, etc.). (The principle is beyond every suspicion of Platonism, since this intermediary sphere is not something ontogenetically archetypical, but nothing other than an historical product, a cultural given.)

I have added that within the "intermediary" sphere, along with the "social," "cultural," *fixed* contents we must recognize the "subjective," *variable* contributions, either in the form of personal empirical data that fill word outlines with experience, or subjective concepts, or intimate psychological elements, or connotative emotional facts.

It remains, now, to specify that my perspective puts the accent on the fact that intermediary "conceptual systems" in no way exhaust the real, even if culturally they tend to give that impression. "Systems" and "models" simply construct relationships out of the world's infinite availability. Speaking of scientific "models," Enrico Bellone recently said (1973, 16):

> From the beginning of the nineteenth century, the production of scientific knowledge developed by criticizing every representation of the so-called "external world" which sought to reduce the real to an immutable block of things, given once and for all and characterized by an external absoluteness; the criticisms that science has addressed to this image have always brought forth more evidence that the so-called "external world" may rather be a dynamic organization which systematically escapes every attempt at explanation founded upon criteria of absolute truth, whatever the degree of internal coherence of such attempts may be.

The "model," then—including the "model" produced by art that does not differ, in procedure, from other types of modelization—does not "explain" the object, which is never reducible to the subject, and is never to be conceived as the elusive shell of an ultimate and eternal "hidden structure" (for which categories of knowledge cannot be absolute, but flexible and relative), but simply *organizes the object* and constitutes a *vision* of it. It could simply be defined as *a systematic opening of the intellect and the senses to the world* (without any implication of ontological truth). Its "cognitive" power consists in the fact that it shows *how to see* an object, and therefore allows things to be seen that *were not seen before*.

The conceptuality of language would have to be seen, therefore—to recur to a metaphor dear to the General Semantics school[1]—as a "map" with respect to the territory to which it refers. The map is indispensable for finding one's way around the territory, but cannot be identified with it. Continuing the metaphor, I'll say that the history of culture consists in a continuous variation of the map, with reorderings, accumulations of detail, destruction, and reconstruction, all intended to satisfy the contingent heuristic demands of the culture itself.

4.1. The situation therefore appears to be as follows: the conceptual screen of language determines our experience of the world, but it is also altered, modified, enriched, specified, by nonlinguistic experience. Although one cannot negate the hegemonic position language assumes in cultural systems—above all, because all other systems can be translated into language, and further because it is principally to language that a culture entrusts the transmission of its own contents—it is nevertheless undeniable that language is not the only system of modelization. There are forms of knowledge that are not linguistic.

In a very interesting article—limited, however, to the visual world alone—Greimas mentions the point of view of neopositivist logicians, according to whom signification is constituted by a reference of "proper names" to the world's objects, and to the point of view of the linguists, who in general point to the incidence of language in their constructions and significations. He then goes on to insist upon the malaise of the major part of those who have seen the material universe exhausted within the closed universe of linguistic concepts. (It might be recalled that Peirce and Morris attributed to language a function that not only represents the world, but *creates* it directly.) He suggests that in addition to a semiotics of natural languages, it is necessary "to postulate the existence of a semiotics of the natural world and to conceive the relationship between signs and linguistic systems, on the one hand, and signs and systems of signification of the natural world on the other, not so much as a reference of the symbolic to the natural . . . but more as a network of correlations between two levels of signifying reality" (1970, 52).

Undoubtedly the position of linguistic radicalism that idealistically exhausts the world in language, with its two fundamental theses—the one of "linguistic determinism" (language determines thought) and the other of "linguistic relativity" (every language realizes a definite vision of the world)—invokes some specification. It is true that language determines thought, but it is also true that thought, as conceptual result of experience, determines language. Every day, modern semiotics produces examples of structurations and non-linguistic systems that, in much the same way as natural language, establish units—that is, they segment the *continuum* of the world—they bring elements into relation with each other, structure them into systems, and fix them as values.

4.2. These illuminations, then, reflect upon the material world to show it as a complex of semiotic systems. Greimas states that a "common characteristic of natural signs," that of "directing to the other from the self" (1970, 53), together with the idea (stemming from cultural typology) that these constructive and cognitive systems allow delimitation of cultural areas insofar as they represent "types" of culture, necessarily lead us to accept the thesis that in *any case one speaks of systems of signs*, even though there is an exception that we shall see shortly. Thus, when we refer to the rapport between the world of the *literary work* (of art, in general) and the *extraliterary world*, we must speak above all of a *relationship among systems*.

In the first place, given that the literary work is a linguistic phenomenon—and given further that the non-linguistic semiosis of the world is commonly translated into the semiotic system of language—the relationship *work/world* will be fundamentally constituted by the rapport between *literary language* and *natural language* (besides, of course, the rapport between *literary language* and *other literary languages*), a relationship, this, that has long been recognized, even by those who have thought along different lines. Literary language, for example, was spoken of as *écart* in comparison with standard language (Spitzer, 1948; Devoto, 1950, etc.).

But in the second place, and in the light of what I have sustained above, it must be observed that this rapport is not sufficient and exhaustive. The system of the literary work is not comparable only with that of natural language, but also with all *other* cognitive systems which are not necessarily translated in the common language system but rather are often in contrast with it, and are potentialities of its transformation from stale, closed ideology to up-to-date, open ideology. Further, the literary work can express semiotic systems, not yet present in the culture, which the work reveals by means of *its own* modelizations. Literature is at the same time "systematic" and "modelizer," in the sense that "it actualizes systems" (collective) but also proposes "models" (singular). An attentive observation of the phenomenon "art," in general, will indicate the importance that unclearly systematized "margins" assume. Lotman recognizes these, as we have said, around distinct centers of culture, and, just because they are peripheral, amorphous, or unknown, these limits show the subsistence of a portion of the world beyond cultural codification, a residue of great semiotic systemizations. Among its diverse activities art includes the venture into these indistinct confines of the world. To say that language structures the real should not—as we have said—necessarily imply that the structuration is complete and exhaustive. The real allows—even invokes—further structurations beyond the culturally given.

4.3. To my mind, then, the thesis closest to the truth will be constituted by a third position that, along with that of the logicians and the radical linguists, will moderate oppositions. Such moderation is made possible, however, by admitting the possibility of non-linguistic experience, according to which reality is intuited as objects, classes of objects, and relationships among objects not yet nominated and established, but that invoke nomination and structurization. In knowing the world, then, dialectical exchange between direct experience and linguistic mediation, between linguistic and non-linguistic structurations is possible. This takes nothing away from our recognition of the formidable function of language, which becomes *not only the point of departure, but also the point of arrival*, of knowledge, thus constituting an indispensable apparatus of psychic, sensorial, and intellective organs, and the fundamental means of segmenting the *continuum* of the world and of establishing differences and relationships among things.

This position is also supported by various criticisms of the "linguistic relativity" hypothesis, which is identified in the perhaps arbitrary association—all things considered—of Whorf with

Sapir.[2] It has been objected that in his conception of language Whorf was too tied to verbal atomism, obscuring the fact that the signified is not so much constituted by the value of the single word but by complexes and relationships of words (the word itself—as Wittgenstein specified—assumes a precise value only in context), and that, in theory, word complexes can express, in all languages, the shadings of which he speaks.[3] A language may not have words that designate "snow that falls," "snow on the ground," "muddy snow," "packed snow," or "snow that flies pulled by the wind," distinctions that the Eskimoes possess (Whorf, 1971, 216)—but any language may, on occasion, express such concepts and can do so by means of its own locutions, if not otherwise than in the particular uses of a poetic language that creates appropriate segmentations, distinctions, and relationships, even if such designations, within the boundaries of a specific culture, do not constitute an ordinary social need. This observation is particularly important with regard to poetry, which seeks to make subtle and delicate distinctions of this kind. The value of poetic language lies precisely in the fact that it has expressive possibilities that do not belong to standard language. It is in this sense that Mallarmé opposed the language of poetry to the language of the "tribe."

Thus, even with all its recognizable dilettantism, Korzybski's thesis assumes a certain validity, although we cannot share his principle of a completely prelinguistically structured reality: language is always insufficient with respect to the real, the "map" always incomplete with respect to the territory to which it refers, because in the real, as in the "territory," there are infinite possibilities of observing reliefs, levels, and gradations that had not been considered in conventional linguistic conceptuality.

4.4. In such a perspective, the scientific, philosophic and artistic activities that have been separated and opposed with such care naturally begin to come together again; all formulate constructive hypotheses of the real. It is commonly said that scientific hypotheses always function to verify practice, while artistic hypotheses subtract themselves in principle from every possibility of verification. But is it really true that the latter cannot be verified? This is also a point that must be attentively discussed in an effort to overcome certain prejudices that aesthetics has long entertained.

It is well known that linguistics has never been comfortable with the idea of reference, so much so that the major part of its conceptions leave out the sign-referent rapport as a question that belongs to peripheral fields of investigation. Semiotics has also pushed away the problems of referentiality, as Umberto Eco has categorically done in his delimitation of its specific field. And there is no doubt—as has already been pointed out—that Eco is right, given that his discourse attempts to found a science, and a science cannot be founded without establishing epistemological limits. But can the semiologist of literature found a science of literature—or even a theory of literature—on the basis of an analogous delimitation? It would be to isolate literature in a sterile vacuum that would reduce its function to that of a "semiotic technique" (while the "user" of literature does not receive a "technique" but its "effects") or to restrict its function to one of mere diversion, without recognizing the fundamental values that tie it to experience, to feeling, to ideas of the world, and even in some cases to their transformations. The decadent principle of art for art's sake, a phenomenon torn away from life, is quite overdone. With all probability it reflects—as has been observed—nothing more than a typically bourgeois attitude that, by means of such a relegation of art into pure ideal, conjures away every effusiveness on the practical level.

The meditation on literature's "autonomy" has also contributed to the conception of a literature separate from the world. There was talk, in fact, of "autosufficiency," "autoreflection," and so on, concepts that—as we shall see—are not to be abandoned, but neither are they to be taken as absolute. Too often—to refer to times nearer at hand—we are reminded of the Jakobsonian formula of the literary message's "autoreflexivity," forgetting that Jakobson himself proposed it as a principal, but not exclusive, characteristic of literature.

Recently, Paul Ricoeur (1975), reconsidering the problems of the poetic sign and remembering the teachings of Nelson Goodman (1968), energetically sustained the necessity for a *denotative theory of metaphor*. Not only "saying," but also "representing" is referential. A painting *denotes* the real as much as a scientific discourse. The metaphor (understood, naturally, in a wide sense: the work is itself a "global metaphor") sinks the primary sense (impossible) to let *another perspective* rise to the surface. This too is referential and, as such, is liable to "verification." By destroying literal sense, the poem renews sense that does not remain closed in the sphere of poetic discourse but provokes a new referential horizon. Such references do have a hypothetical nature ("suspended referentiality," 278) but one that, fallen into an extraliterary context, is recognized as "true" or "false" ("metaphoric referentiality").

To go back to the distinction between "signified" and "sense," again proposed by Antonino Buttitta and Mario Giacomarra (1972), the "signified" of signs becomes "sense" when the sign has fallen into the socio-cultural context: "The sense of a sign is given by its relationship with a determined extralinguistic situation; it depends, that is, upon the function that a signifying set performs in the heart of a situation" (32). Transferring this concept to our consideration of literary work, recognized and studied in its original historical context, or in later, diverse historical contexts, we can simply say that *the verification of a work's referentiality* lies in whatever "sense" it demonstrates at the moment of reception. To have a "sense," and not only a "signified" (which, with a maximum of historico-philological approximation can always be reconstructed) means that some connections have been made with the referents that belong to the receiver's socio-culture. The above-cited authors conclude as follows:

> It is thus from an investigation into the situation, inasmuch as it is a socio-cultural context, that the sense of a word, a gesture, a work of art emerges. Just as society promotes the creation and use of an historically determined language, so only knowledge of the socio-

cultural context will allow us to further semiotic investigations, beyond the moment of the simple signified (32).

This, to my mind, is the way to found a semiotics not only of the *signified*, but of the *referent* as well.

4.5. These concepts of "metaphoric referentiality" and "sense" open, as we see, a clear perspective on the question of the work of art's referentiality but, according to the directives of our discourse, the phenomenon can be further specified.

I spoke above of an intermediary sphere (Weisgerber's "Zwischenwelt")—hereinafter referred to as (Z_1)—constituted by the conceptual plane of language, a conceptual plane that is placed between the subject's knowledge and the world, and gives to this latter order and sense, insofar as it is a determinant of experience. But we have also added that the autonomous experience outside language (E) is a determinant of language itself, just as is the other non-linguistic conceptuality constituted by the semiosis of the natural world (Z_2). Now, in literary language one verifies naturally the same conceptual function with regard to the real that one recognizes in natural language and in the semiosis of the natural world, but the conceptual plane of literature is *another conceptual plane* (Z_3) equipped with its own laws, *that establishes a triple rapport* with (Z_1), (Z_2), with (E):

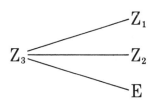

From one point, the conceptual plane of literature *refers* to the world organized by common language and by the modelizations performed by philosophy and science (Z_1), from another, to the world of natural semiotic systems (Z_2), from still another, directly to empiria (E), with operations that explore zones which are not culturally systemized, denoting the non-denoted. By means of such neologistic operations, literature inserts itself into cultural "vacuums," offering itself as an extremely refined means of picking up shades of meaning, of creating "words" for the most subtle and linguistically unexplored experiences. And in that sense it returns to the origins of the world, upsets the ordinary denomination of "natural language" and "artificial language," inverting their values. "Artificial" language becomes, if anything, standard language.

With this conception of relationships, (Z_3) becomes an experience field organized in itself that reflects and clarifies world situations and can also constitute itself as a new and opposing systemization, different both from that of ordinary language and that of natural semiosis and science.

If what we have said is true, we see that at the level of the rapport with the extraliterary world, literature also activates an "introjective doubling" symmetrical to that of the other two vertices of the communication model expounded in the first and second chapters. In its complexity, the phenomenon can be schematized as follows:

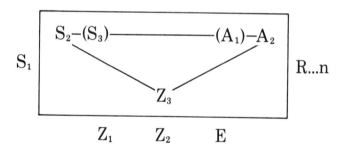

S_1 = external author (sender 1)

S_2 = implicit author (sender 2)

S_3 = second narrator—occasionally present[4] (sender 3)

A_1 = internal addressee—occasionally present

A_2 = prefigured internal addressee (who can also be identified with A_1)

$R \ldots n$ = external receivers

Z_1 = conceptual plane of standard language

Z_2 = conceptual plane of the natural world's semiotic systems

Z_3 = conceptual plane of the work

E = marginal experience with respect to cultural systems (linguistic and non-linguistic)

4.6. Perhaps it is still necessary to add something about this and about a possible misunderstanding that could arise from what we have stated up to this point. The possible misunderstanding regards the concept of the "autonomy" of literature which could be subverted if one were to put the accent decisively upon the literary text's "referentiality." However, the concept of autonomy remains valid even if the referential rapport we have been discussing goes back to reconsider the function of art as "mirroring." Undoubtedly, art counts among its activities that of using, in the terms and modes proper to it, the states of the objective world. Art can *also* be—and is—imitation. But at the moment when thoughts, feelings, characters, sensorial data, happenings, and cultural systems enter into structure, these assume a reality that is (a) only *hypothetical*, and (b) obeys laws that are its *own*. Pierre Macherey adduces an elementary example:

The "Napoleon" of whom Tolstoy speaks in *War and Peace* escapes historical criticism. If we read the book attentively, we are aware that the name hardly designates a real person, but has a sense only in relation to the textual set in which it appears. The writer's act . . . raises an object and at the same time institutes the unique evaluation norms to which the given object may be subordinate" (1966, 57).

It will be well to add however that Tolstoy's "Napoleon" is a fantastic hypothesis of the Napoleon of history and is not conceivable without reference to reality. In fact, Macherey himself affirms that art is "autonomous" but not "independent"; "it institutes the difference that permits it to be what it is only by establishing some relationships with what is different from itself" (65, 67).

The autonomy of literature is above all tied to the laws of language. Even when the work proposes to "mirror" or "imitate" a real object—let us say "describe" it—it must not only make "choices," given that not everything can be described, but must also obey lexical and syntactical laws, and must then arrange these choices in syntagmatic order. While the real object is shown in its totality and simultaneity, the literary object is "read" as a complex of relationed signs. It happens thus that the word is *a way of organizing the real*, in the sense that by constituting itself as structure it produces an order that is at once the order of both subject and object. We repeat that the signs of literature do not differ in this from those of natural language. It is only that literature does this on a *non-conventional*, a different level from that of ordinary language, and separates itself from the latter inasmuch as it institutes another conceptual level that is set before the ordinary plane of reference. The referential plane of literature represents a proposal, or project, to organize (structure and give meaning to) the world different from any plan one may obtain by means of ordinary linguistic structures. The plane (Z_3) consequently becomes a fresh experience of things, free from habit, the obtuse and distracted torpor of ordinary experience. It seems to me that this substantially coincides with what Cesare Segre has recently written on the theme of mimesis and lie:

> Departing from reality, fiction renders our perceptions of the real more refined and sensitive, corroborates our critical faculties, reveals, through paradox, forces and motivations. So much the more can the reality from which we exit be truly interpreted by the irreality into which we enter (1978, 185).

In brief, the autonomy of literature is one obtained with the materials of language; but these undergo fresh actualizations and transformations within language itself. And the conceptual plane which they produce does not establish a direct rapport with the contextual situation (natural language is always "in situation") but is separated from direct contextuality, to actuate an indirect rapport—metaphorically referential, Ricoeur would say—that, so to speak, *reproduces* the real on an imaginary and hypothetical plane.

Lazar Osipovič Rèznikov (1964; 1967, 69) has stated that the conceptual plane of language (signified) is constituted by a certain quantity of information surrounding the object (referent), with which it never identifies itself. "The sign designates the object—he says—and expresses the signified" (70). Well, now, still in brief, and in this perspective that substantially coincides with what I have myself indicated, I shall say that the function of art rests in its capacity to furnish a non-conventional quantity of information about its referents.

Conclusion

We are now in a position to summarize the discourse articulated in the foregoing text. *Literature is an "act of systemization" in which we recognize two simultaneously occurring activities: "systematic actualization" and "original modelization"*—(closed and definite or open and suggestive). Further, the distinctive feature which sets literature apart from other "systemizations" and "modelizations" (for example, those of standard language and the sciences) is that it actuates *the introjection of the three exponents of the ordinary communication model.* This phenomenon permits the literary text to be "autosufficient," that is, to constitute a source of communication even without the contextual conditions that are indispensable to ordinary communication. In addition, we can also synthesize our response to Di Girolamo's skepticism with which we initiated the parabola of our discourse.

With regard to "literature," the receiver assumes an attitude characterized by *acceptance of the introjection of referents.* A reader *knows* that the text in hand *has been conceived* in observance of this convention; or, even with regard to a text that originally had a different orientation, s/he may wish to treat it as though it were "literary" and therefore *decide* in any case to observe the rules of the convention.

Said convention is articulated—from the reader's perspective—in the essential points recapitulated below:

a) The receiver knows that the elocutive act is decontextualized, and therefore not to be received directly, but obliquely (since the empirical author is "absent" and therefore cannot establish interlocutory practices with the reader, and since the internal addressee is a preconstituted imaginary subject with whom the reader can, as like as not, identify). Consequently, s/he knows that one cannot use the text as direct signification, and that in its "signified" one is constrained to find a "sense."

b) The receiver does not evaluate the text's referentiality on the basis of a direct verifiability, knowing that fiction and truth are materials to be submitted to another verification, that of "metaphoric referentiality." And s/he does not evaluate the text for its referential power only but also, and contemporaneously, for the *way* in which it actuates the reference that is, itself, a given of the communication.

c) The receiver knows that the text's language can be an arbitrary actualization of *langue*. In such case s/he accepts the arbitrary as norm.

Therefore, the "convention" of "literariness" consists in the particular attitude shared by both producer and receiver of the text or by the receiver of a text not intentionally conventionalized but which nevertheless can be treated as such.

Given that it is lost in the darkness of time, we would not be able to establish the beginning of this convention in our cultural tradition; therefore, while recognizing its historicity, neither would we be able to consider it a cultural variable.

Notes

ONE.
Transmission

1. See also Dressler (1975), Schmidt (1976b), Garroni (1973), and van Dijk (1976).
2. Modern theory on the subject is both copious and unanimous. See Booth (1961), Todorov (1967), Foucault (1969), Kristeva (1970), Rousset (1973), Chatman (1978), Eco (1975), Corti (1978a, 1978c), and Krisinski (1977).
3. See Faccani and Eco, eds. (1969), Lotman-Uspenskij (1975a, 1975b), with Ferrari-Bravo's introductory essay, Uspenskij (1968), Lotman (1970), and finally Żólkiewski (1973, 1974), Bauman (1973), Avalle (1975, 1977), Pagnini (1976), Segre (1977), Cardona and Ferrara, eds. (1977), and Collections and Anthologies (1978a), in particular Miceli, Buttitta, and Corti (1978a).
4. See Groupe μ (1970, 106, et seq.).
5. For an example, see Pagnini (1978b).

TWO.
Reception

1. Recently, various scholars have pointed out the need for this distinction: Barthes (1966), Riffaterre (1971), Iser (1972), Schmidt (1976b), van Dijk (1976), Corti (1978a, 1978c), and Eco (1978).
2. See Fabbri (1973), and Eco (1976a, 135–142).
3. For the concept of "isotopy," see Greimas (1970, 10): "By the term *isotopy* we generally mean a bundle of redundant semantic categories which underlies the discourse we are considering." The "level" is a natural isotopy of the language; while the "isotopy" is a structure within the "semantic levels." See also Corno (1977, 206).
4. In a recent essay (1978), Umberto Eco has reexamined the activity involved in reception of the narrative text.
5. All aspects of the problem have been examined by Genette (1976).
6. See Johnson (1976).
7. As we know, Barthes has put his convictions to the test in his reading of a Balzac text (1970).
8. For a theory of the "macrotext," see Serpieri (1973, 7–43).
9. For the theory, see Contini (1971).
10. For the theory, see Puppo (1964).
11. For the theory, see Russo (1950), Binni (1963).
12. For the theory, see Terracini (1966).

13. For the theory, see Salinari (1962).
14. For the theory, see Mukařovský (1966; 1973, 5–80).
15. For the theory, with various references to Carlo Bo, Oreste Macrí, and Piero Bigongiari, see Ramat (1969).
16. For the theory, see Segre (1970), Pagnini (1970), and Corti (1978c).
17. For the theory, see Corti (1972, 1978c) and Avalle (1975).
18. For the theory, see Frye (1957).
19. For the theory, see Spurgeon (1935) and Clemen (1969).
20. For the theory, see Serpieri (1973, 7–43; 1978c).
21. For the theory, see Orlando (1978, 1979).
22. For the theory, see Beccaria (1975) and Pagnini (1977).
23. See the now classic analysis by Jacques Derrida (1969) of Philippe Sollers's *Nombres* as well as Julia Kristeva's later analysis of the same text (1969, 290–350). See further Stefano Agosti's readings (1972) and his clear methodological synthesis (1978).

THREE.
Dramatic Literature and the Theater

1. A first step toward theater can be seen in "recited literature" ("poetry" or "prose" read before one or more listeners), since the person who recites tends to assume some structures particular to "character." But it's a question of only a first step, given that the non-dramatic text, beyond the fact that it is not in dialogue, does not have precisely those distinctive "deictic-performative" features that countersign theatrical discourse.
2. See further: Bettetini-De Marinis (1977), Ruffini (1978), Collections and Anthologies (1978b), and Ubersfeld (1978).

FOUR.
Reference

1. The reference is to Korzybski (1933) and his followers (S.I. Hayakawa, A. Rapoport, etc.).
2. The locution "Sapir-Whorf hypothesis" is, in fact, a disputable coinage of Whorf's editor, J. B. Carrol (see Whorf, 1956).
3. See also Carlo Tullio Altan's excellent essay (1969).
4. In Conrad's *Heart of Darkness*—to cite only the first example that comes to mind—there are two narrators.

Bibliography

COLLECTIONS AND ANTHOLOGIES
1978a *Strutture semiotiche e strutture ideologiche,* "Quaderni del Circolo Semiologico Siciliano," 8–10 (Palermo: Stampatori tipolitografi associati)
1978b *Come comunica il teatro* (Milan: Il Formichiere).
1978c *Crisi del sapere e nuova razionalita'* (Bari: De Donato).
AGOSTI, STEFANO
1972 *Il testo poetico. Teoria e pratiche di analisi* (Milan: Rizzoli).
1978 "Discorso, parola analitica, linguaggio poetico," in Fornari, F., ed., 1978.
ALTAN, CARLO TULLIO
1969 "Considerazioni sull'ipotesi Sapir-Whorf," *Sociologia* vol. 3, n. 3.
ARNHEIM, RUDOLF
1971 *Entropy and Art: An Essay on Disorder and Order* (The Regents of the University of California).
AVALLE, D'ARCO SILVIO
1969 "Dinamica di fattori anomali," *Strumenti critici* 10; revised and amplified edition in Caprettini, G.P., and Corno, D., eds., 1979).
1972 *Corso di semiologia dei testi letterari* (Turin: Giappichelli).
1975 *Modelli semiologici nella Commedia di Dante* (Milan: Bompiani).
1977 "Da Santa Uliva a Justine," in Veselovskij-Sade, 1977.
BALLY, CHARLES
1932 *Linguistique générale et linguistique francaise* (Bern: Francke).
BARILLI, RENATO
1974 *Tra presenza e assenza* (Milan: Bompiani).
BARTHES, ROLAND
1966 *Critique et vérite* (Paris: Seuil).
1967 *Système de la mode* (Paris: Seuil).
1970 *S/Z* (Paris: Seuil); English trans. *S/Z* (Cape, 1967; Hill and Wang, 1977).
1973 *Le plaisir du texte* (Paris: Seuil); English trans., *The Pleasure of the Text* (Cape, 1967; Hill and Wang, 1977).
BAUMAN, ZYGMUNT
1973 *Culture as Praxis* (London: Routledge and Kegan Paul).
BEACH, JOSEPH WARREN
1932 *The Twentieth Century Novel: Studies in Technique* (New York: Appleton-Century).
BECCARIA, GIAN LUIGI
1975 *L'autonomia del significante. Figure del ritmo e della sintassi* (Turin: Einaudi).
BELLONE, ENRICO
1973 *I modelli e la concezione del mondo nella fisica moderna da Laplace a Bohr* (Milan: Feltrinelli).

BENE, CARMELO
1977 "Intervista a C. Bene," *Scena* 2.
BENVENISTE, EMILE
1939 "Nature de signe linguistique," in *Acta Linguistica*, no. 1.
1958 "De la subjectivité dans le langage," *Journal de Psychologie*, July-September; now in Benveniste, 1966.
1966 *Problèmes de linguistique générale* (Paris: Gallimard); English trans. *Problems in General Linguistics* (University of Miami, 1970).
BETTETINI, GIANFRANCO, and DE MARINIS, MARCO, EDS.
1977 *Testo e communicazione* (Florence: Guaraldi).
BINNI, WALTER
1963 *Poetica, critica e storia letteraria* (Bari: Laterza).
BOOTH, WAYNE C.
1961 *The Rhetoric of Fiction* (Chicago and London: University of Chicago Press).
BRAUDEL, FERNAND
1958 "Histoire et sciences sociales; la 'longue durée,'" *Annales-Economies Sociétés Civilisations*, XIII, no. 4, October-December.
BREMOND, CLAUDE
1973 *Logique du récit* (Paris: Seuil).
BÜHLER, KARL
1934 *Sprachteorie* (Jena: Fischer).
BUTTITTA, ANTONINO
1978 "Formalismo semiotico e semiotica della cultura," in Collections and Anthologies, 1978a.
BUTTITTA, ANTONINO, and GIACOMMARRA, MARIO
1972 "Preliminari su significato e senso," *Humana* 7, *Quaderni degli Istituti di Etnologia e Geografia della Universitá di Palermo* (Palermo: Stampa luxograph).
CAPRETTINI, G. P., and CORNO, D., EDS.
1979 *Letteratura e semiologia in Italia* (Turin: Rosenberg and Sellier).
CARDONA, G. R., and FERRARA, E., EDS.
1977 *Messaggi e ambienti* (Rome: Officina Edizioni).
CASETTI, FRANCESCO
1977 *Semiotica*. Critical essay, evidence, documents (Milan: Edizioni Accademia).
CATALANO G., ED.
1974 *Teoria della critica contemporanea. Dalla stilistica allo strutturalismo* (Naples: Guida).
CHATMAN, SEYMOUR
1974 "La struttura della communicazione letteraria," *Strumenti critici* 23 (translated from the English); now in Chatman, *Story and Discourse; Narrative Structure in Fiction and Film* (Ithaca: Cornell University Press, 1978).
CLEMEN, WOLFGANG

1969 *Das Drama Shakespeares* (Gottingen: Vandenhoeck und Ruprecht).

CONTE, GIAN BIAGIO
1974 *Memoria dei poeti e sistema letterario: Catullo, Virgilio, Ovidio, Lucano* (Turin: Einaudi).

CONTE, MARIA-ELISABETH, ED.
1977 *La linguistica testuale* (Milan: Feltrinelli).

CONTINI, GIANFRANCO
1951 "Preliminari sulla lingua del Petrarca," *Paragone*, April; now in Contini, 1970.
1970 *Varianti e altra linguistica* (Turin: Einaudi).
1977 "Filologia," in *Enciclopedia del Novecento* (Istituto dell'Enciclopedia Italiana, Vol. II: Rome).

CORNO, DARIO
1977 *Il senso letterario: Note e lessico di semiotica della letteratura* (Turin: Giappichelli).

CORTI, MARIA
1972 "I generi letterari in prospettiva semiologica," *Strumenti critici* 17.
1976 *Principi della communicazione letteraria* (Milan: Bompiani).
1978a *Il viaggio testuale. Le ideologie e le strutture semiotiche* (Turin: Einaudi).
1978b "Modelli e antimodelli nella cultura medioevale," *Strumenti critici* 35.
1978c *An Introduction to Literary Semiotics* (Bloomington: Indiana University Press).

CRESSWELL, see HUGHES

CURRELI, M., and MARTINO, A., EDS.
1978 *Critical Dimensions: English, German and Comparative Literature. Essays in Honor of Aurelio Zanco* (Cuneo: Saste).

CURTIUS, ERNST R.
1953 *European Literature and the Latin Middle Ages*, tr. Willard R. Trask (London: Routledge & Kegan Paul).

DEESE, JAMES
1965 *The Structure of Associations in Language and Thought* (Baltimore: Johns Hopkins University Press).

DE MARINIS, see BETTETINI

DERRIDA, JACQUES
1969 "La dissémination," *Critique*, February-March.

DEVOTO, GIACOMO
1950 *Studi di stilistica* (Florence: Le Monnier).

DI GIROLAMO, COSTANZO
1978 *Critica della letterarietá* (Milan: Il Saggiatore).
1981 *A Critical Theory of Literature* (Madison/London: University of Wisconsin Press).

DIJK, TEUN A. VAN

1972a *Beitrage zur generativen Poetik* (Munich: Bayerischer Schulbuch-Verlag).

1972b *Some Aspects of Text Grammars: A Study in Theoretical Linguistics and Poetics* (The Hague: Mouton).

1976 "Pragmatics and Poetics," in Van Dijk, ed., 1976.

DIJK, TEUN A. VAN, ED.

1976 *Pragmatics of Language and Literature* (Amsterdam: North Holland P.C.).

DRESSLER, WOLFGANG

1972 *Einfurung in die Textlinguistik* (Tübingen: Niemeyer).

DUNCAN, HUGH D.

1953 *Language and Literature in Society* (Chicago: University of Chicago Press).

EBERLE, OSKAR

1955 *Cenalora, Leben, Glaube, Tanz und Theater der Urvolker* (Oltan: Otto Walter).

ECO, UMBERTO

1968 *La struttura assente* (Milan: Bompiani).

1973a *Il segno* (Milan: ISEDI).

1973b *Tutto il mondo è attore* (radio interview), Terzo Programma (Turin: ERI Edizioni 2/3).

1975 *Trattato di semiotica generale* (Milan: Bompiani).

1976a *A Theory of Semiotics* (Bloomington: Indiana University Press).

1976b "Codice," in *VS* 14; now in *Enciclopedia Einaudi*, vol. 3, 1978.

1978 "Possible Worlds and Text Pragmatics: 'Un drame ben parisien,' " *VS* 19/20.

1979 *The Role of the Reader* (Bloomington: Indiana University Press).

ELAM, KEIR

1977 "Language in the Theater," *Sub-Stance* 18:19.

ESCARPIT, ROBERT

1958 *Sociologie de la littérature* (Paris: Presses Universitaires de France).

FABBRI, PAOLO

1973 "Le communicazioni di massa in Italia: sguardo semiotico e malocchio della sociologia," *VS* 5.

FACCANI, R. and ECO, U., EDS.

1969 *I sistemi di segni e lo strutturalismo sovietico* (Milan: Bompiani).

FERRARI-BRAVO, DONATELLA

1975 "Sistemi secondari di modellizzazione," in Lotman-Uspenskij, 1975.

FORNARI, F., ED.

1976 *Psicoanalisi e istitutizioni* (Florence: Le Monnier).

FOUCAULT, MICHEL

1969 "Qu'est qu'un auteur?" *Bulletin de la Société Francaise de Philosophie*, July-September.

FREGE, GOTTLOB
1892 "Uber Sinn und Bedeutung," *Zeitschrift fur Philosophie und philosophische Kritik* 100.
FREUD, SIGMUND
1922 "Psychoanalysis," in James Strachey, ed., *The Standard Edition of the Complete Psychological Works of Sigmund Freud*, vol. 18, p. 235, (London: Hogarth Press, 1953–1966).
FRYE, NORTHROP
1957 *Anatomy of Criticism, Four Essays* (Princeton: Princeton University Press).
GARRONI, EMILIO
1973 "Immagine e linguaggio," in *Documenti di lavoro, Centro Internazionale di semiotica e di linguistica di Urbino* 29.
GENETTE, GÉRARD
1972 *Figures III* (Paris: Seuil).
1976 *Mimologiques: Voyage en Cratyle* (Paris: Seuil).
GIACOMARRA, see BUTTITTA
GOODMAN, NELSON
1968 *Languages of Art* (Indianapolis, New York: Bobbs-Merrill).
GREIMAS, A. J.
1968 "The Interaction of Semiotic Constraints," *Yale French Studies* 41 (now in Greimas, 1970).
1970 *Du Sens* (Paris: Seuil).
GROEBEN, NORBERT
1972 *Literaturpsychologie: Literatur Wissenschaft zwischen Hermeneutik und Empirie* (Stuttgart: Kohlhammer).
GROUPE μ
1970 *Rhétorique Génerale* (Paris: Larousse).
GULLÍ PUGLIATTI, PAOLA
1976 *I segni latenti. Scrittura come virtualità scenica in "King Lear"* (Messina-Florence: D'Anna).
HAUSER, ARNOLD
1958 *Philosophie der Kunstgeschichte* (Munich: Oscar Beck).
HUGHES, G. E., and CRESSWELL, M. J.
1968 *An Introduction to Modal Logic* (London: Methuen).
INGARDEN, ROMAN
1960 *Das literarische Kunstwerk* (Tübingen: Niemeyer, 2d ed.).
ISER, WOLFGANG
1970 *Die Appellstruktur der Texte: Unbestimmbheit als Wirkungsbedingung literarischer Prosa* (Kostanz: Universitat-verlag).
1972 *Der implizite Leser: Kommunikationsformen des Romans von Bunyan bis Beckett* (Munich: Fink).
JAKOBSON, ROMAN
1960 "Linguistics and Poetics," in *Style in Language*, ed. T. Sebeok (Cambridge: MIT Press), now in Jakobson, 1963.
1963 *Essais de linguistique générale* (Paris: Minuit).
1973 "The Dominant," in Tzvetan Todorov, ed., 1973.

118   *Bibliography*

JAUSS, HANS ROBERT
    1967 *Literaturgeschichte als Provokation der Literatur-wissenschaft* (Kostanz: Universitats-Druckerei).
JOHNSON, ANTHONY L.
    1976 "L'anagrammatismo in poesia: premesse teoriche," in *Annali della Scuola Normale Superiore di Pisa* IV,2.
KORZYBSKI, ALFRED
    1933 *Science and Sanity. An Introduction to non-Aristotelian Systems and General Semantics* (Lakeville, Conn.).
KOTT, JAN
    1964 *Shakespeare nostro contemporaneo* (Milan: Feltrinelli); Italian trans. of *Szkice o Szekspirze* (Warsaw, 1961).
KOWZAN, TADEUSZ
    1968 "Le signe au théatre, Introduction á la sémiologie de l'art du spectacle," *Diogène* 61.
KRIS, ERNST
    1952 *Psychoanalytic Explorations in Art* (New York: Schocken).
KRYSINSKI, WLADIMIR
    1977 "The Narrator as a Sayer of the Author," *Strumenti critici* 32–33.
KRISTEVA, JULIA
    1969 *Recherches pour une sémanalyse* (Paris: Seuil).
    1970 *Le texte du roman* (The Hague-Paris: Mouton).
LACAN, JACQUES
    1977 *Écrits: A Selection* (New York, London: W.W. Norton & Company [paperback]); English trans. (partial) of *Écrits* (Paris: Seuil, 1966).
LOTMAN, JU. M.
    1967 "Il problema di una tipologia della cultura," Italian trans. of "K probleme tipologii kul'tury," *Trudy po znakovym sistemam*, in Faccani and Eco, eds., 1969).
    1972 *La struttura del testo poetico* (Milan: Mursia), Italian trans. of *Struktura chudozestvennogo teksta* (Moscow: Iskusstvo, 1970).
    1977 *La cultura come mente collettiva e i problemi della intelligenza artificiale*, "Documenti di Lavoro e prepubblicazioni del Centro Internazionale di Semiotica e di Linguistica" (Urbino, September, Series A), Italian trans. of *Kul'tura kak kollektivnyj intellekt i problemy iskusstvennogo razuma (Predvaritel'naja publikacija)* (Moscow: Akademja nauk SSSR [Naucnyj sovet po kompleksn oj problemy "kibernetika"]).
LOTMAN, JU. M., and USPENSKIJ, B. A.
    1971 "Il meccanismo semiotico della cultura," in Lotman-Uspenskij, 1975a; Italian trans. of "O semioticeskom mechanizme kul'tury," *Trudy po znakovym sistemam* III (Tartu); "Sul meccanismo semiotico della cultura," in Lotman-Uspenskij, 1975b.
    1973 "Mito — Nome — Cultura," Italian trans. of "Mif — Imja —

Kul'tura," *Trudy po znakovym sistemam* (Tartu), in Lotman-Uspenskij, 1975a, 1975b.

1975a *Tipologia della cultura*, ed. R. Faccani and M. Marzaduri (Milan: Bompiani).

1975b *Semiotica e cultura*, introductory essay and translation by D. Ferrari-Bravo (Milan-Naples: Ricciardi).

MACHEREY, PIERRE
1966 *Pour une théorie de la production littéraire* (Paris: François Maspero); English trans. *A Theory of Literary Production* (Routledge & Kegan Paul, 1978).

MANNONI, OCTAVE
1969 *Clefs pour l'Imaginaire ou l'Autre Scène* (Paris: Seuil).

MARCHESE, ANGELO
1976 *L'analisi letteraria* (Turin: SEI).

MICELI, SILVANA
1978 "Semiotica dell'ideologia e/o ideologia della semiotica," now in Collections and Anthologies, 1978a.

MOLINARI, CESARE
1978 "Appunti per una storia del Repertorio," *Quaderni di teatro* I, 1 August.

MUKAŘOVSKÝ, JAN
1966 *Studie z estetiky* (Prague: Odeon); Italian trans. *Il significato dell'estetica* (Turin: Einaudi, 1973).

ORLANDO, FRANCESCO
1978 *Toward a Freudian Theory of Literature* (Baltimore: Johns Hopkins University Press).

1979 *Lettura freudiana del "Misanthrope" e due scritti teorici* (Turin: Einaudi).

PAGNINI, MARCELLO
1970a "Per una semiologia del teatro classico," *Strumenti critici* 12; now in Raimondi and Bottoni, eds., 1975.

1970b "La critica letteraria come integrazione dei livelli dell'opera," in *Critica e storia letteraria, Studi offerti a M. Fubini* (Padua: Liviana Editrice), now in Catalano, G., ed., 1974.

1974 "Il sonetto (A. Zacinto): Saggio teorico e critico sulla polivalenza funzionale dell'opera poetica," *Strumenti critici* 23, reprinted in Marchese, 1976 and in Caprettini and Corno, eds., 1979.

1976 *Shakespeare e il paradigma della specularità* (Pisa: Pacini).

1977 "Il testo poetico e la musicalità," *Linguistica e Letteratura* II, 2.

1978a "Riflessioni sulla enunciazione letteraria e in particolare sulla communicazione a teatro," now in Collections and Anthologies, 1978b.

1978b "Il demoniaco poesco: Saggio di psicoanalisi letteraria," in Currelli and Martino, eds. (Cuneo: Saste).

PEIRCE, CHARLES S.
1931–35 *Collected Papers* (Cambridge: Harvard University Press).

PRINCE, GÉRARD
1973 "Introduction a l'étude du narrataire," *Poétique* 14.
PROPP, VLADÌMIR J.
1928 *Morfologija skazki* (Leningrad: Academia); English trans. *Morphology of the Folktale* (Bloomington: Indiana Research Centre in Anthropology, 1958).
PUPPO, MARIO
1964 *Il metodo e la critica di B. Croce* (Milan: Mursia).
RAIMONDI, E., and L. BOTTONI, EDS.
1975 *Teoria della letteratura* (Bologna: Il Mulino).
RAMAT, SILVIA
1969 *L'ermetismo* (Florence: La Nuova Italia).
RÈZNIKOV, LAZAR OSIPOVIĆ
1964 *Gnoseologiceskie voprosy semiotiki* (Editions of the University of Leningrad); Italian trans. *Semiotica e marxismo* (Milan: Bompiani, 1967).
RICOEUR, PAUL
1975 *La Metaphore vive* (Paris: Seuil).
RIFFATERRE, MICHAEL
1971 *Essais de stylistique structurale* (Paris: Flammarion).
ROUSSET, JEAN
1973 *Narcisse romancier: Essai sur la première personne dans le roman* (Paris: Corti).
RUFFINI, FRANCO
1974 "Semiotica del teatro: recognizione degli studi," *Biblioteca Teatrale* 9.
1978 *Semiotica del testo, l'esempio teatro* (Rome: Bulzoni).
SADE, cf. VESELOVSKIJ
SALINARI, CARLO
1962 "La critica marxista," *Ulisse*, Anno 15, vol. 3, fasc. 47.
SANTINI, L.R., and RAIMONDI, E., EDS.
1978 *Retorica e critica letteraria* (Bologna: Il Mulino).
SAPIR, EDWARD
1921 *Language* (New York: Harcourt Brace).
SARTRE, JEAN-PAUL
1948 *Qu'est-ce-que la lettérature?* (Paris: Gallimard); English trans. *What is Literature?* (London: Methuen, 1950).
SCHMIDT, SIEGFRIED J.
1976a "Towards a Pragmatic Interpretation of Fictionality," in van Dijk, ed., 1976).
1976b *Texttheorie* (Munich: Fink).
SCHÜCKING, LEVIN L.
1961 *Soziologie der literarischen Geschmacksbildung* (Bern: Francke).
SEGERS, RIEN T.
1978 *The Evaluation of Literary Texts* (Leiden: The Peter de Ridder Press).

SEGRE, CESARE
  1970 *I segni e la critica* (Turin: Einaudi).
  1974 *Le strutture e il tempo* (Turin: Einaudi); English trans. *Structures and Time* (Chicago and London: University of Chicago Press, 1979).
  1977 "Cultura e sistemi di modellizzazione," in *Semiotica e Cultura* (Padua: Liviana Editrice).
  1978 "Divagazione su mimesi e menzogna," in Santini, L.R., and Raimondi, E., eds., 1978).
  1979 *Semiotica filologica: Testo e modelli culturali* (Turin: Einaudi).
SERPIERI, ALESSANDRO
  1973 *T.S. Eliot: le strutture profonde* (Bologna: Il Mulino).
  1977 "Ipotesi teorica di segmentazione del testo teatrale," *Strumenti critici* 32–33; now in Collections and Anthologies, 1978b.
  1978 "Sul concetto di trasformazione e sulla poetica generativa," now in Collections and Anthologies, 1978c.
SPITZER, LEO
  1948 "Linguistics and Literary History," in *Linguistics and Literary History: Essays in Stylistics* (Princeton: Princeton University Press).
SPURGEON, CAROLINE
  1935 *Shakespeare's Imagery and What it Tells Us* (London: Cambridge University Press).
STAROBINSKI, JEAN
  1974 *Trois fureurs* (Paris: Gallimard).
STENZEL, JULIUS
  1934 *Philosophie der Sprache* (Munich-Berlin: R. Oldenbourg Verlag).
STYAN, J. L.
  1971 *Shakespeare's Stagecraft* (London: Cambridge University Press).
TERRACINI, BENVENUTO
  1966 *Analisi stilistica* (Milan: Feltrinelli).
TODOROV, TZVETAN
  1967 *Littérature et signification* (Paris: Larousse).
TODOROV, TZVETAN, ED.
  1973 *Questions de poétique* (Paris: Seuil).
UBERSFELD, ANNE
  1978 *Lire le théâtre* (Paris: Editions Sociales).
USPENSKIJ, see also LOTMAN
USPENSKIJ, B. A.
  1968 *Principles of Structural Typology* (The Hague-Paris: Mouton).
VAINA, LUCIA
  1977 "Les mondes possibles du texte," *VS* 17.
VESLOVSKIJ-SADE (Veselovskij, Aleksandr Nikolaevic, Marquis de Sade)
  1977 *La fanciulla perseguitata*, D. S. Avalle, ed. (Milan: Bompiani).

1977 "Les mondes possibles du texte," *VS* 17.

VESLOVSKIJ-SADE (Veselovskij, Aleksandr Nikolaevic, Marquis de Sade)

1977 *La fanciulla perseguitata*, D. S. Avalle, ed. (Milan: Bompiani).

VOLLI, UGO

1978 "Mondi possibili, logica, semiotica," *VS* 19/20.

WEISGERBER, JOHANN L.

1962 *Von den Kraften der deutchen Sprache*, vol. 1, *Grundzuge der inhaltbewogenen Grammatik* (Dusseldorf: Schwann).

WHORF, BENJAMIN LEE

1971 *Language, Thought, and Reality*, ed., John B. Carroll (Cambridge, Mass.: The M.I.T. Press).

WUNDERLICH, DIETER

1971 "Pragmatik, Sprechsituation, Deixis," *Weitschrift fur Literaturwissenschaft und Linguistik* 1–2).

ŽÓLKIEWSKI, STEFAN

1973 "Des principes de classement des Textes de culture," *Semiotika* VII, 1.

1974 "Quelques problèmes de sémiotique de la culture dans les ouvrages d'auteurs des pays est-européens" (Unpublished communication read at the First Congress of the International Association of Semiotic Studies (Milan, 2–6 June).

Index